AF325836

STOLEN CHILD

Marie-Claire ViDja
Olivier Goujon

STOLEN CHILD
Subjected to Family Violence

Afterword by Anaïs Biehler, lawyer at the Lyon bar

Max Milo
TÉMOIGNAGE

Max Milo, Paris, 2023

www.maxmilo.com

ISBN : 9782315011896

To my daughter, to my brothers and sisters in tears and arms.

To Vikhram and Sadou.

Your children are not your children.
They are the sons and daughters
Of the call of life to itself.
They come through you and not from you.
Well, let them be with you,
They do not belong to you.

Khalil Gibran, "Your Children.

Warning

In order to preserve anonymity and respect the privacy of individuals, names and locations have been changed.

Thanks to Marie-Claire

"It takes two to remember," says Virginie Efira to Benoît Magimel in *Revoir Paris*; thank you, Olivier, I couldn't have asked for a better co-author.

Thank you also to Marie-Servane, Jean-Charles, my daughter, the CMP psychology team, the Psys du Coeur, SOS Amitié, all the beautiful people of my family, the authors, the readers and the supporters of the cause... Thank you to Anaïs for her support and her trust. Thank you all for believing in us, in me, and thank you for your past and future support of the EVRP. Finally, thanks to the Barlu girls.

Prologue

"Shut your mouth and dig!

- To bury the books?"

Whenever an "impromptu" police raid is planned in the neighborhood, he is warned by his spies, and we have to hide the videos and newspapers he receives from Afghanistan. He orders me to dig a hole in the garden to put the garbage bags containing the propaganda material. When the police have finished their "visits", I dig again to collect everything. But I'm a little surprised because I haven't heard anyone mention the police coming. And then, usually, I dig a well; this time, I have to dig deeper and wider. A rectangle. I'm afraid, and my hands hurt.

"There, are you okay?"

He looks at me in silence, lifts me up by the neck and throws me into the hole. Before I can get up, he joins me and presses his foot on my chest to keep me down: "The whores, we slit their throats, but you, I'll bury you alive."

My name is Marie-Claire. I'm 48 years old and I'm fine, but my life hasn't always been easy.

1.
The hell of my nights

> "However, if an event becomes imprinted in the intimate
> memory of a person, it is because it has been brought to light
> by the emotional reactions of those around him
> or by the importance which the culture allots to it.
> Boris Cyrulnik, *Un merveilleux malheur*,
> Éd. Odile Jacob, 1999.

I run. A man catches up with me. It is my uncle Noury. He knocks me down, crushes me with all his weight, lifts me up and pinches me against a dirty wall. I try to escape again, but his hands, as large as flippers, grab me just below the throat and lift me up. I don't touch the ground anymore. He squeezes. I am going to die. At the edge of the sidewalk, I see my grandmother Yemma. Behind her, the sea. Yemma opens her mouth and lets out a long, shrill cry that stops my murderous uncle's gesture. Noury lets go of me. I tell myself that he is going to take it out on my grandmother. I am angry at myself for abandoning her, but I am too afraid. I run. Shitty night.

My awakenings are an ordeal. Hours sometimes, to get out of the pain of a night that leaves me wrapped in anguish. To soften an arm, to feel again my legs, to shake my ankylosed bust... And my bones crack, and my muscles refuse... Then I remain lying down, the eyes with the ceiling, to make up my body and my spirit: I am a single woman, French, and Algerian by force, I have a 25-year-old daughter named Laure, a job as a contractual and temporary teacher-researcher who struggles to make up for the abyss of the rent of a two-room apartment in an old working-class district of Paris and a life that is mostly chiche and worried.

Here I am, I put one foot out of bed, I draw the curtain, it is gray. At the moment, I am giving a course at the École des ponts et chaussées: "History of the Arab revolutions in the 19th century". We say "at the Bridges". But today I don't have a class. On the other hand, I have an appointment at 10 a.m. with the physiotherapist and at noon with the shrink.

My phone vibrates. It's a message from Pearl, she wants to accept the marriage, "of course". I answer immediately: "Think about it, where you are, it will be very difficult to divorce if you get married, you will have papers but that will not allow you to come back to France. Where are you with your request for a birth certificate?" While I'm answering, another message arrives, it's Joseph: he still hasn't gotten his passport back and he got caught going through his father's secretary. He doesn't say anything more, but I understand why I hadn't heard from him for several weeks: his father has beaten him up again.

I have had nightmares almost every night since I was 11 years old. Before that, I don't know. For the past few months, it's often this one, which I call my re-kidnapping. I'm working on escaping them but they haven't diminished in frequency or intensity. Shower, breakfast, for a long time date makrouts and milk, now coffee with milk and Gerblé cookies, kiwis if I'm in funds. It takes me another hour to prepare. For eight years now, Laure has been living with two girlfriends. From time to time, she comes back home for a few weeks, when she travels abroad or when she changes roommates. I'm always a little upset when she leaves, but I'm careful not to show it. We have our mother-daughter rituals, and I really like that. Laure is a *data scientist* for a large French company in the energy sector. And *deejay*. She loves her job, which she learned through an engineering degree, an internship in the United States and an exchange program in Mexico, but what she loves most is composing and scratching while watching people dance. I go to her performances whenever I can, I love it. I like to be among the youth. I'm a party girl.

Laure is my best reason to get up in the morning.

My biological mother's name is Annie. I call her my genitrix. She was born in the fifties in Burgundy. When she was 14, she met a 26 year old man, my father. Immediately, it degenerates. He was twelve years older, Algerian, atheist and without any real profession, let's say vaguely a mechanic, but above all he was a dreamer, a bit of an anarchist with no other goal in life than to live and let live. At that time, Pépé and Mémé, Annie's parents, who are called Marcel and Julienne, are a truck driver and a midwife. She is a Catholic, he is an alcoholic. They are strict with their four children, to say the least. The truth is that the blows fly without being asked for and without making anyone jealous, even if my mother takes a little more than the others, no doubt. Later, there will be some for me too. They live in a small village whose name I have forgotten, close to a big city in Burgundy. Pépé was in the Algerian war. He is often sad. Naturally, when my mother told them she was pregnant, they began by beating her up. Then they throw her out. Finally, in the meantime, there are arguments, runaways, other beatings, a complaint lodged against my father - my mother is not 15 years old when she meets dad and hardly 16 when the infamy happens!- who went to prison for six months in 1975. Most likely, he wasn't around when I was born. I'm not sure. On

1. The hell of my nights

the street with a newborn baby and her atheist dreamer, my mother had little choice but to start working. Just after my birth, she found a small job as a pharmacy employee and then another as a hostess in a movie theater. She probably already hated me. At the time of the birth, she chose to have me born under X, then retracted, I don't know why, perhaps because it was not done. I do know, however, that she carried me to her parents' village and laid me in swaddling clothes outside the church. Perhaps she imagined that this is what one does when one does not want a child but was too stupid to think of it before? Perhaps she believes, like any farm girl in Bresson's movies, that her life as a woman is lost before it begins? Perhaps, but I doubt it, she has read Victor Hugo and imagines herself as a wandering and miserable Fantine? Yes, perhaps she saw in the spiral of events the fulfillment of some calamitous destiny? No doubt, the times and her education did not dispose her well, she simply did not think that far, all in her instinct of repulsion against fate, life, men, her parents and me.

But here I am, in the midst of the chaos of his youth.

You have to live with me.

By chance and rain, it was Pépé himself who found me on the porch of the church where he was running to take shelter after leaving the café. With Mémé, they decided to call their daughter back and to organize a life together in the pretty house they owned at the entrance of the village. The living together lasted two days before they kicked us out. For good, this time.

Hacène, my father, came from Annaba, a large city on the east coast of Algeria. One day, Pépé will explain to me that before the war it was called Bône and that it was so pretty, with its beaches and white houses, that it was nicknamed "la Coquette". I will think about it often when I am there. Hacène's real name is Abdelkrim, but he changed his name. Abd-el-Karim is "the submissive to the Generous" in Arabic.

The Generous is one of the hundred names of Allah. Hacène is "the good one", more secular, it surely suited him better. I have a photo of him in Jijel in 1962 and another in Paris in 1965, so he arrived between the two but I don't know exactly when. I do know when he returned, it was just a few months after my birth. He had just been released from prison. As he had some savings, he moved my mother and me into a small apartment in Burgundy, then to Lyon. In the big city, we would be happier. Hacène is happy that I am part of his life. He is a dreamer. And as he is a dreamer and a bit of a mechanic, he opens a small garage in an empty room under the apartment. He leaves his last reserves there but a future is taking shape: the Dauphine and the four-wheelers invade the cities, they will have to be repaired. He will be there for that.

Hacène is happy that I exist and he wants to take me to see his family in Algeria. No way, my mother is against it. He will leave alone to announce his happiness in the country. For the garage, no problem, he entrusts it to his friend Mouloud, they emigrated together and know each other since childhood. In the village, the welcome was certainly good. He stays a few weeks. Too many. When he returned to Lyon, he discovered that his childhood and emigration friend had taken his place in Annie's life. This is a terrible blow for Hacène who sincerely loved Annie and her boyfriend. In despair, he returns to Algeria where he is welcomed this time with the dishonor of a cuckold. He fell into depression and then became insane. His family had him locked up. Later, they will say to me that he was going to repeat my name, that he was setting Annie's and my place settings at the table, that he did not wash himself anymore...

In Lyon, Mouloud is doing well. He manages the garage and our life. Lazy, he doesn't know much about mechanics, but he's in it for a few years before the business collapses. Mouloud might then look for work. But, very quickly, we had to leave the small apartment that my father had found to shelter our happiness. We headed for the Croix-Rousse hill, which Annie called "Croix-Rouge". The memories of my early life with Mouloud are rare but clear. I know that he is not my real father, but when I insist on knowing more, Annie evades. I don't insist anymore. I will not know who my biological father is. Mouloud is away most of the week. I don't know where he goes; to work, I'm told. On weekends, he meets us. I also remember a vacation in Corsica where people are naked. I don't understand immediately and I am afraid. Mouloud and my mother explained to me that here it was possible to live without clothes. I will have other experiences like this. I hate it. But my most vivid memory is of Bangkok. I don't know why we are going there, although I understand that we are not on vacation. My mother's face is worried. Mouloud is not there. On the spot, we meet a man who is introduced to me as his brother. He buys me an Orangina. We take a cab. I have the eyes widened, the traffic is a tight skein of bicycles and small cars with three wheels. On the sidewalks, people harangue the passers-by by holding out to them bowls and steaming skewers, one shouts, one is active, the city swarms and rustles without respite. In the middle of the agitation, we stop in front of a building with very high walls, like a castle. At the entrance, an iron door with two wings. Mouloud's brother comes down with papers in his hand. I ask Annie where we are, and she answers straightforwardly:

"It's the prison, we're going to get Mouloud.

- Why is he in prison?" She looks at me with an indefinable air. Even today I wonder about the meaning and scope of that look. There is arrogance, like defiance in front of the fear that she knows how to inspire with her answers:

"Mouloud is in prison for drug trafficking."

I don't know anything else. I will never know anything else about this episode. We enter a wing of the building; the ceiling is high; on the left, a wall with inaccessible windows, on the right, rooms with bars and men behind the bars. One cell is occupied by women, many women, and many children around them. Everyone is looking at us. We arrive at Mouloud's cell. I don't recognize him, with his long hair and beard. He reaches through the bars to grab my Orangina. I step back. Annie orders, "Give it to him. I nod, she snatches the bottle out of my hand and hands it to him, but it doesn't fit between the bars, she is forced to hand it back to me. It's my Orangina. The brother speaks:

"You're going to stay here with Mouloud, your mother and I have to go to the office."

Before I can even react, I see them walking toward a door at the end of the hall. The brother has a suitcase in his hand that I didn't see when he got out of the cab. He won't have it when he gets out. I am alone in this wide, empty corridor, with all these men clinging to the bars and staring at me. Some of them make signs to me, they speak in an incomprehensible language, the same as the kebab sellers. "Don't be afraid," Mouloud tells me, but I am terrified, almost as much by the presence of so many curious men as by the appearance of the only one I know. I fear that the bars will suddenly open and arms will grab me and carry me into the evil darkness of their lair. I still dream of this episode. Fortunately, the door opens, Annie and the brother return. My mother calmed me down. A man in uniform opens the cell. Mouloud leaves. We get back in the car and leave the prison. At the hotel, his brother tells Mouloud to wash himself. In the hotel lobby, we wait for him while he gets a haircut. Then we go to eat on a boat. I am reassured. I have no memory of the night, probably at the hotel. But in the morning I hear a lively discussion between the three of them. The brother is angry: "You're crazy, I'll take care of it, stay here", he says to my mother. He goes out, Mouloud and Annie do not speak. I am in a small bed. We wait. When he comes back, the brother says, "It's settled," but I can still hear them arguing loudly. They do not agree. We take a cab to the airport, then a plane. Annie is in a bad mood but she doesn't speak. Nobody tells me anything. I ask: "Are we going home?

- Yes, we're going home," the brother replies. I don't know what that means, I'm suspicious:

- In Lyon?

- Shut up."

We landed in Algiers, but I didn't know it was Algiers. Nobody told me, I found out by deduction, by recognizing the places and the people, much later. During the flight, I asked several times why we weren't going back to Lyon, but I always got the same answer: "But you're going to shut your mouth!" I understand that the brother orders Mouloud and Annie, I wonder why. Annie ends up explaining to me that we are going to see some family members.

I have no memory of the arrival, but I remember a house by the sea. Mouloud's brother is called Moustafa. Mouloud is in the bathroom, vomiting. A lady is kind to me. We go to bed. The next day, Annie leaves without us. They explain to me that Mouloud is sick and needs to be treated. I have no idea how long we will be there, but I think we will stay for several weeks, probably several months. Mousse's wife, Kima, is very nice to me. I also remember that we often eat cakes in the living room and that there is a huge hallway where we go shopping with my cousins. At the end of this big corridor, there is the studio where Mouloud keeps the bed. From time to time, I look through the half-open door, it worries me a little to see him lying like that. Finally, one day, I find him at the table with us and we eat normally. He is better, I am told.

My next memory is at home, in Lyon. I slept for a whole day. I went back home.

2.
Between the knife and the piano

"It can't be true that all this happened to me, or someone would come to my rescue," and the patient prefers to doubt the correctness of his judgment rather than believe in the coldness of our feelings, our lack of intelligence, in short, our stupidity and wickedness."
Sándor Ferenczi, *Le Traumatisme*, Éd. Payot, 1982.

My beginning of the week is therefore invariably medical-professional. That is to say that it is organized around my classes and appointments with the various repairers of my body and mind. This frees up the weekends for my personal reconstruction and my thousand projects. On Mondays, I see the physiotherapist and the shrink. On Tuesdays, the psychomotrician. Once a month, I have an appointment with the head shrink of the Center. And I try to fit the rest of my little health problems in between. This week, it's very busy: check-up of my pituitary micro adenoma, long COVID treatment, neurological diagnosis to be confirmed...

I guess I'll have to put off my ulcer until next week again.

"The most difficult thing is to be believed. We don't often believe women, so women who have experienced what I have experienced..." As I don't like to lie down, I sit in front of the psychologist of the CMP (Medical and Psychological Center) and I pour out my heart, it does me good. I got a place in January. The care is free. I see him once a week. And I wonder a lot. Are we repeating what we went through? Why do I always do the same crap? Where does this taste of death come from? Why do I have to go through all these physical problems on top of the moral hell I went through? Will it ever stop? These are some of the questions that still remain unanswered. But I am moving forward. For the first time in a long time, I feel like I have a perspective.

As for anyone else, the place of excavation is childhood. Except that I didn't have the childhood of anyone. To say the least. Yesterday I took the Holmes and Rahe test[1] . Anyone can do it, it can be found online, and all you need is a little memory and counting skills. In order to determine a kind of stress scale, these two Harvard researchers drew up a list of the many traumatic events in a person's life that could affect him or her in one year: death of a loved one, sexual violence, internment, drugs, serious illness, etc. Each event is assigned a number of points. Each event is assigned a number of points that are added up at the end. A total of 200 is an alarm signal, at 300 they advise heavy treatment, possibly hospitalization. I chose some years of my life, 1985, 1995, 2003, 2007, 2019... My annual total oscillates between 800, the good years, and 2000, the bad ones... As a result, I stopped adding up. Much too stressful.

---

1. Thomas H. Holmes and Richard H. Rahe are two Harvard University research psychologists who have been interested in the physical impact of stress on the bodies of victims over time. Their list was updated in 2007 by the psychologist of "psychogenealogy" (see chapter 4), Anne Ancelin Schützenberger.

First half of 1980

After Mouloud brought me back, asleep, from Algiers to Lyon, life resumed. I am too small to ask myself all the questions: who are the people we spent all that time with in Algeria? Is Mouloud sick? Why did my mother leave me all this time? Where was she? Why doesn't her body answer me when I hug her when I come back?

In Lyon, we no longer have the garage. Mouloud drinks. At first I don't understand, but very quickly I make the connection between his mood swings - he can kiss me and push me away in the same gesture, smile at me and then get angry... - and the fact that I see him through the PMU window, almost every day, on my way home from school. Sometimes, when it's really late, Annie sends me to pick her up. I walk to school. I really like school. I have friends there and it feels like a safe place where the teachers and kids are happy. I feel safe there.

The arrival of Fleur, my first sister, in the family, fills me with joy. Mouloud and Annie also seem happy. Annie has gentle gestures when she changes her, she doesn't speak loudly to her, she takes her in her arms. She is like a mother. And I like to watch my sister smile.

But one day we leave. Mouloud tells me that the apartment has become too expensive, that we should leave it. In fact, Annie tells me that Mouloud has gambled away the family's money at the races! "So we're going to find another apartment," I ask. I see the truck parked in front of our house again. We load our stuff in it in bulk, our whole little life. I don't have many toys, they fit in a bag that Annie puts in the back of the truck, under the seat. Mouloud explains me that we are going to leave with this vehicle. But where to? Where to? Mouloud smiles, and Annie says, "Nowhere. I am very worried about his answer, what do you mean, nowhere? Do we

2. Between the knife and the piano

have to go somewhere? What about school? What about my friends? What about the Red Cross? We leave. I discover it along the roads and in the villages: we do not go anywhere. We drive from one town to another, mostly small towns. We wash ourselves at the fountains or in the public baths. It was 1980. I remember election posters. I have notebooks to work in, I don't do so bad, I think. I often ask to do homework but Annie says, "Who cares?" One day when I ask her to make me recite my tables, I get a slap. Mouloud drives all the time. Without Annie asking me anything, I decide to stay next to him to keep him awake because we often drive at night. And Mouloud is drunk all the time. I'm afraid, I can't take my eyes off him. What torments me the most, during these months of wandering, is obviously missing school, but it is, beyond that, the idea that we are not "like everyone else". I understand that the people around us, those we pass and that I observe from a picnic table on the side of the road, from the sidewalk of a supermarket or from the window of the Citroën truck that shelters us, these people of the world we cross without belonging to it, have a normal life, a job, a house, friends. We, we do nothing but drive, Clermont-Ferrand, Valence, Mulhouse... During the day, we sleep on the benches or on the side of the road. Do we run away? Are we hiding? I will never know. However, for me this wandering will stop. One day, without being told, I realize that we are returning to Lyon. Mouloud is driving. But we don't go to our old house. He stops at the station. Annie explains to me that we have to separate. Mouloud will stay with Fleur, my sister. I have to go with my mother. I ask where we are going. Annie says, "Nowhere. We take a train. She remains silent. After several hours, we get off the train. I read "Besançon" on a big blue sign. We go to my Aunt Alice, Annie's sister. Well, I go, because Annie doesn't even enter the house when my aunt opens the door. She greets Alice, who seems surprised to see us, then turns back without looking at me. I am standing there on the doorstep. I think I'm crying.

I stayed with my aunt for quite a long time, more than a year, I think. It's a beautiful period. She lives with Riky, he is a friend of Dad's and Mouloud's and Annie's too, but he works, he does normal things. My aunt is an artist, she paints and creates lampshades and paintings with butterflies and sheep's wool, which she sells at the markets. She even has a place at the Christmas market in Strasbourg. I know she wanted to be a photographer, but Pépé didn't want to, it was too expensive and Alice "didn't need to study!" It is cold in the Jura. I am in first grade, there are about ten of us in my class. My cousin Adène is in the same school, but in kindergarten. He is nice, I give him my hand to cross the road and we share a snack. The school is a big building with a sloping roof. In the playground, there are high trees and covered areas where we take shelter when it rains or snows. I get a little lost, even though it is much smaller than in Lyon. I don't know the teacher or my new friends, but I immediately feel the same sense of security. In the end, as long as it takes me to adapt, I will feel as comfortable at school as I did at my aunt's house. But one day, Annie, Mouloud and Fleur come back to get me. Without warning. Annie is pregnant up to her eyes. We go back to Lyon. When we are almost there, we have an accident because of an apple. Annie wants to grab one from the basket at her feet but the fruit is rotten. She gets angry, says she doesn't like rotten apples and wants to throw it out of the window, but for a few days the window is blocked, we don't know why. Annie opens the door, Mouloud swerves, Annie falls on the sidewalk and I fall backwards inside the van. Mouloud screams and slams on the brakes, but too late to avoid a wall. My next memory is of Mouloud taking a cloth, pressing on Annie's head and yelling at me to get my sister out of

2. Between the knife and the piano

the car. I lift Fleur out of her bassinet and carry her down to the running board just as the engine catches fire. The engine had been smoking a lot for the past few days, Mouloud told the police. Annie's head is open and dark matter escapes. The firemen arrive. It is the end of 1980, or the beginning of 1981. At that point, I have no more memories until we leave the hospital: Annie has given birth to my second sister, Rose, her head is bandaged, she is pushing the baby in a baby carriage. We cross the street. A car comes too fast and hits Annie and the baby. My little sister is fine but Annie's foot is broken. Back to the hospital. We come out a few days later. I wonder where we will live because the van is broken. Mouloud says that he made it repair. But we don't stay in Lyon. We go to Mauguio, near Montpellier. I don't know why we are going there, but I understand that we don't have to stay in Lyon. I'm glad we don't have to drive all the time because I don't trust Annie and Mouloud. They do drugs. I don't understand it precisely, but I see that they are often wobbly, that they don't have much strength and that they often sleep. I won't put words to their behavior and daily acts of addiction until much later. But I understand that this is what caused us to have this accident, rather than the apples.

The Citroen van is all broken. I don't know how we got to our new home.

In Mauguio, the house is on one level. There is a bay window in front. The kitchen and the living room are connected. Behind it there is a small corridor that leads to Annie's room, on the left, which is also mine, she "arranged" a corner at the end of the room for me. The other room was big enough for the three of us to stay in, but she reserved it for Fleur and my new little sister, Rose. We have a garden in front, which is quite small, and another one in the back. The house is next to the cemetery. I often go there to play. The house overlooks the road and, beyond, a much larger public garden. And in the middle there is a river. I often go to see it before going to school. I'm happy to be back in class. I haven't fallen behind, despite my life on the road, my interruptions and my time in the Jura. In addition to my regular classes, I am doing theater. One time I'll be playing a cowboy in the end-of-year performance, and another time an Arabian dancer. And also a fairy. I also do pottery, paper mache masks like in Venice, silk painting and scarves. I am happy, I feel like I am following in the footsteps of my aunt Alice.

Annie and Mouloud continue to take drugs, but at least we are not on the road anymore. Mouloud drinks a lot, but Annie doesn't. Many people come by the house. Men mostly. There are bags of cannabis stashed all over the front yard. In the back, near the cemetery, the big garden is full of cannabis plants surrounded by sunflowers. I've seen a lot of people staggering around Mauguio, a lot. Mouloud is there on weekends, but during the week he is almost always away with his new car. In the evening, Annie hangs cannabis from the ceiling in several places in the house, a little in our bedroom, but mostly in the hallway and the living room, to dry. When it's dry, my sisters and I have to crumble it and put it in little jars. Then, I am sometimes in charge of carrying the jars to a house in the village to a certain George. One day, the village policeman saw me enter George's house: "So, little one, are you going to George's house again? My memories blur, I'm not sure how the story ends but I go to the station. Then he takes me home. Annie talks with him and, as soon as he leaves, she comes to get me in the room where I have taken refuge. I get slapped. I have another memory of the police. I am on the train with Mouloud. The train stops, or is it at the station? I don't know anymore. Anyway, police trucks are parked along the street... or along the track. Some policemen get into our car, I understand instantly that it is us they want. In fact, they arrest us. Mouloud is handcuffed. We get off the train, everyone looks at us and I feel ashamed. They put us in the van. At the station, I have my Maya the Bee record with me, the one Mouloud gave me. The policeman questions me. I am standing on a long bench, almost at his level. He asks me to think carefully, he wants to know what we did, whose house we went to, if we saw anyone in the city. But I know absolutely nothing. I suggest him to "ask Mouloud instead". So he takes my Maya the Bee record and breaks it over my head. I am 8 years old, maybe 9. I don't know if the facts are connected anymore, but I also have the memory of burning cannabis plants and police officers watching. Mouloud went to prison several times, I think, but he never stayed long.

I like Mauguio, but Annie hits me a lot. I am an embarrassment to her, I feel it, I know it, but I don't know what to do about it. She has always been brutal with me and I took a lot of slaps very early. But in Mauguio, it's becoming a hell. I know I can't trust the woman who gave birth to me, but now I'm just beginning to understand that she hates me. Instinctively, it upsets me, I feel that it is against nature, and especially that it is unfair. She is my mother. I should be able to rely on her at the slightest change in my life, but that is impossible. Children's brains don't understand the hostility of their immediate environment, I will learn later.

One night, I get up to pee, I see Annie with a man. I have no choice but to walk past her bed to the bathroom. I am tetanized. I feel like the man is beating her, but he's not. I don't understand what they are doing. She looks at me, he turns around. I run to the bathroom. She joins me: "You're doing it on purpose, aren't you? To embarrass me, to embarrass me." She grabs me by the neck and drags me into the garden. She strangles me. I pass out. I wake up at dawn because I have dew under my nose, and then my neck hurts a lot. A friend

I like lives behind the public garden. We are bench neighbors and I have already been to her house, her parents are normal. I go to her door and wait for someone to open it. I'm back asleep when the father comes out to go to work. They let me in and give me breakfast because I'm hungry, as usual. I tell them everything. They look at my neck and put ointment on me. They talk among themselves, I hear the word police and I get scared. I understand that my family is going to be in trouble. I don't want to. They took me to the police station but asked me not to say that I had been to their house. They are afraid of Mouloud, I think, and of all the people who come to the house. A policeman listens to me. Then another one takes me to the school. I was late, but he spoke with the teacher. In the evening, I go back home after having hung out a lot in the streets to delay the moment of meeting Annie. When I arrive, she rushes after me. She was worried that I wouldn't come back from school, so she called the police who told her to wait. But I shut down completely. I refuse to say where I was and if I saw the police. She hits me and then orders me to stay in the room. I fall asleep and I am in a lot of pain. The next morning, she drags me into the bathroom. She turns on the faucet and holds me under the spray. It is cold. She chokes me. This is the first time. This will become a kind of ritual: several times a week, I feel like it's every day, she'll grab me while I'm still asleep, order me to run to the bathroom to wash myself, and then enter. She will stand behind me, look at me in the mirror, grab my neck and squeeze, then suddenly release. Each time, I will think I am dying. This will last until I am kidnapped. To this day, the shower worries me to the point that I still get rashes because I can't close my eyes to protect them from the soap. It's a budget in soothing eye drops! Sometimes she also bites me until I bleed. While she does it, she blows, I hear her rage, like a dog. Sometimes I have her head very close to me and

2. Between the knife and the piano

I want to hit her but I hold back because I know it would be worse afterwards. Other times, she drags me around the yard by my hair. She can also beat me by surprise. One day, while I was sitting on the couch watching TV, without any warning, she pulled my head back and jammed it against the doorframe of the living room, then slammed the door several times. When I regain consciousness, she tells me it's because I put the plaid on the couch wrong.

My sisters and I go to the same school, but we don't eat at the canteen every day. It is Annie who tells us before leaving who has to come back for lunch. One lunchtime when she made steaks and mashed potatoes, my favorite dish, she forbids me to eat because I didn't set the table properly: "You get up, give your meat and go put your plate in the sink." I put the knife in the drainer, she tells me again: "Not like that" I start again, it's still wrong, I start again, still wrong, I don't understand what I have to do... "Do you want us to get hurt? Do it again!" Yet I put the knife next to the others in the same direction. She tells me that I am a little idiot. She gets up, takes the knife, and sticks it in my arm. I have an opening of four centimeters. She has to take me to the hospital because it bleeds so much. To the nurse, she says that I fell by accident, I don't dare to speak. I miss school. Another time, she crushed a lit cigarette on my wrist. It burns to the bone. It will take years for the skin to recover. She always calls me "bougnoule", "dirty Arab". She also often tells me that I am not funny, that I have prevented her from studying. Once, she yells at me: "You are crazy like your father. Then I ask, "Who is my father?"

A teacher helps me. He knows about the difficult situation at home, and sometimes I go to him to do my homework. I also play with his children. Once, in the schoolyard, I hear him say to another teacher, "The poor little ones, they are screwed up, when they could be fine, but they have crazy parents." It gives me a funny feeling,

I think it pisses me off, but I like that someone realizes that something is wrong with my family. I feel ashamed too.

I ask to register for piano lessons; they are given at the town hall and it is free. Annie accepted. I was offered a very small piano with which my teacher proposed to me to make a small representation. I performed in front of my classmates. It was a great joy.

And then the bikers arrived.

3.
Hostage

"It's nothing at all", "Nothing happened", "Don't think about it anymore" [...] These things are simply covered by a deathly silence, the slight hints of the child are not picked up, or even rejected as incongruous, and this with the total consensus of all those around him and in such a systematic way that, faced with this, the child gives in and can no longer support his own judgment."
Sándor Ferenczi, *Le Traumatisme*, Éd. Payot, 1982.

Every day I receive messages from the children of the shadows. They are children without a presence, ghosts that society ignores. Children who are victims of parental abduction do not exist. At least, not legally. They fall into the categories of children who are victims of violence, kidnapped, in danger... but parental abduction, if it is obviously contemplated by French law, as "illicit displacement of a child abroad", does not establish any specific status for the child, yet parental abduction represents a category in itself of child kidnapping, with a context, a history, processes, criminal constants, that a better definition of the phenomenon can only help to understand. Because "to name things wrongly is to add to the misfortune of the world[2]", to name these little victims wrongly is to add to their misfortune every moment.

In 1989, the UN General Assembly unanimously adopted the Convention on the Rights of the Child (CRC), with the notable exception of Somalia, which had no state, and the United States, because the text contained a paragraph specifying that children could no longer be sentenced to death. This text sets out four fundamental principles: non-discrimination, the best interests of the child, the right to live and develop, and respect for the child's opinions. The context and the course of my abduction in Algeria contravene these four principles (and all the rights related to them[3]), although they are legally binding and ratified by Algeria in 1993. This shows how little attention States pay to them.

In order to give children who have been abducted by a parent an identity and protection, I created the association ThéraVie ARP-APA anti-RPicide in 2021[4]. The first step is to make the general public and political authorities aware of the problem and to create the legal status of child victim of parental abduction (EVRP) recognized by national and international authorities, NGOs, the UN, the Hague Court, UNICEF... Then, once this crime is officially considered as a crime, it will be necessary to create the EVRP law which will "frame" the children during their abduction and help them in their eventual return, and will assure them, afterwards, a

---

2. Albert Camus.

3. Among the 54 articles are the rights to be protected, cared for, rescued, to go to school, to be able to play...

4. RP refers here to "parental abduction". The name of the association, its logo, its slogan and its World ARP Anti-RPicide Day every April 19th are officially registered: ThéraVie ARP-APA International ANTIRPICIDE Anti-Rapt-Parental * Anti-Parental-Abduction. Site: https://www.theravie-arp-apa-antirpicide.org/ Linksights: https://linksight.me/theravie and https://linksight.me/antirpicide Instagram, Twitter and TikTok accounts: mc_arp_apa and FaceBook: Théravie ARP-APA.

real social follow-up. Thousands of children are abducted every year in the world. More than five hundred children[5] disappear every year from France under these conditions, and hundreds of cases, in particular, have been in dispute between Algeria and France since the 1980s. In October 2020, the Chancellery admitted to knowing three hundred and eighteen files[6] "whose management is very difficult", in other words, blocked files that no one, beyond the families, cares about anymore. Considering the average duration of an abduction, estimated according to the files at seven to eight years, how many accumulated files are really at an impasse? How many abducted children, on the other hand, do not appear in this accounting, simply because the parents have not declared the abductions? I have dozens of them at the association, how many are there really? Who cares?

I myself am just one of those files.

Today, I start a new shift at Unesco. I find it hard to take the subway. My feeling of oppression is permanent in transport and closed places. I am afraid of dying. Today's class is "Beginning Arabic Language". Some of the students know my story and sometimes talk to me about it at the end of class, always with delicacy. I have an ambivalent relationship with Arabic. I think it is for me what French was for Kateb Yacine[7] : a catch of war. It is a beautiful, rich, deep, poetic language... but it is the language of my ordeal. And each word

---

5. The association Droit d'enfance lists, for 2021, 43,870 missing children in France, including 545 parental abductions, the vast majority of which are international abductions. The association specifies that this figure is greatly reduced because many parents do not file complaints or are not listed in the FPR (Fichier des personnes recherchées).
6. Figure quoted in the article "Parental abduction abroad, they fight for the return of their children", Ambre Lepoivre, Esther Paolini for BFM TV, 14-10-2020.
7. Kateb Yacine (1929-1989) is an Algerian writer and director who writes in both languages. Anticolonialist, he is studied in Algeria but also in France and is notably in the program of the Comédie française.

brings me back to my past. To my past in 1981, for example, when we went to Algeria for the second time after the "stopover" on our way back from Thailand.

August 1980

Mouloud and Annie are getting married and they want it to happen in Algeria, Mouloud's country. So the ceremony takes place at the French consulate in Annaba. I think they plan to settle there, or at least to stay for a few months. We then moved to Telemly, a beautiful district of Algiers, in a large duplex apartment, precisely located above the French consulate. From the balcony, you can see the monument to the martyrs, the port and the sea. They enrolled me in school. The apartment is nice, but the newlyweds argue all the time. One day, I am astonished to see Annie throwing the plates from the top of the stairs.

We returned in 1981, after Rose was born. My sisters and I sleep in the same room, huge, well furnished, with a small playroom and another one furnished with a wicker lounge. I don't mind the neighborhood. We often go out for a walk along the waterfront. We go to the beach. One weekend, we drive to Annaba to visit a brother of Mouloud. Not the one who came to Thailand, another one I don't know. We stay several days. There is another man in the meeting, who scares me because he stares at me. I tell Mouloud, who abruptly tells me off. And then there is Haya, who is introduced to me as a family friend. She talks in a low voice with Mouloud, then she comes to me smiling: "We're going to go for a walk, I'll make you meet a lot of cousins." I don't want to go, but Mouloud urges me: "I have to. So we go to her house, it's quite far. We settle down in the garden and Haya tells me that I will stay for several weeks: "It will be like a vacation. I burst into tears and call for Annie. Haya, I will learn years later, is the sister of my biological father. I stay for one term, change schools again. I know nothing about the "agreement" between Mouloud and Haya. Mouloud returned to Algiers to find Annie and the girls. And then, one day, he comes back to get me and we go back to Mauguio. At the time, everything escapes me, but with the years and the hindsight, I will understand that it is about a first kidnapping, or about an attempt, on behalf of Mouloud and my mother, to get rid of me... I don't understand why they came back for me either.

In Mauguio, life goes on as before, unfortunately. I am happy to be back. But my daily life became even harder. In 1983, one morning, Annie asked me to come back for lunch. Just me, not my sisters. This never happens. We don't eat at the canteen every day, but most of the time the three of us go home. Sometimes my two sisters come home. I never go home alone at lunch. It's too unusual and it worries me, but I think about it and I tell myself that I'll have my mother all to myself, it's very rare. In fact, she is nice when she gives me the instructions in the morning and still nice when I come back at noon. She lets me eat quietly and a lot. It's pureed meat. Everything is fine, too fine. After the meal, she asks me to sit on the sofa with her. I am on my guard, something is going to happen. Annie takes a pencil and paper and starts to draw. She draws well. A few months ago she got a contract with a movie producer to create cartoons, but it didn't work out, maybe she didn't keep the contract. The drawing she shows me is of a man and a woman embracing. The sexes are visible. I am very uncomfortable. And here she starts to explain to me how one makes love, "so that you are not dumb, so that you know..." I was stunned. First of all, I already have a pretty good idea of how to make love; there was that man last month that I caught

3. Hostage

with her, and then Mouloud and her never hide, I've seen them so many times, in the van and elsewhere! I want her to remove this drawing from my eyes but she holds me. Suddenly, the sound of an engine fills the room. Two motorcycles arrive. I recognize the sound. A classmate showed me a sticker book and I became enamored with Harley-Davidsons. So I hear them pull up to the front door. Annie doesn't seem surprised. They are on the patio with their helmets in hand, I think I've seen them before. I get up and say I have to go to school. She grabs my arm, "You are staying home this afternoon." I look at the picture, I understand what's going to happen to me, so while she goes to greet her friends, I run into the bedroom, open the window and run away. I arrive at school like a fury. At recess, my teacher asks me why I was so late. I just say that my mom wouldn't let me come back to school. He sighs, "This time I'll go talk to her." I say no. He insists. In the evening, when I come home, he is at my place. Annie explains that she found me sick and preferred to keep me. I don't say anything. Later, she questions me, she knows that I ran away because I suspected what would happen to me. She told me that she wanted to teach me, so that I would have experience.

"What is 'experience'?" I asked.

- Well, drawing is theory; to learn, you have to do it, that's experience.

And so that's why the bikers came, to give me experience.

- You don't understand that I take care of you, so that you become a happy woman! It's better that it happens with people I trust and in my presence, so you are safe. But you don't understand anything. You are not funny."

I am not 10 years old. I still have no idea of the relationship my mother had with these two men. My therapists and my co-author will ask me if there was any exchange of money. I do not know anything about it.

A few days later, Annie asks me to bring a bouquet of flowers and bamboo to the chapel hall, where a party is taking place. The place called "the chapel" is a small desecrated church, now a party hall owned by the town hall. It is close to the public garden, two steps from our house. We regularly hear the rumor of celebrations there, often weddings. When I arrive with my bouquet, I push the door and I immediately feel a strong sense of anxiety. Many men are present and I feel that their eyes are all on me at the same time. I don't like this. I spot one of the few girls, I approach, she smiles at me and takes my flowers. What kind of "experience" does Annie want me to do again? What am I doing here? I tell the girl I am afraid. A man pulls me towards him, I say:

"No, I'm going home, you're all grown up!

He emphasizes:

- Your mother told us you had to stay."

I run away. I arrive at home crying, as much of fear as of anger at Annie's new betrayal. When I enter the living room, I run without stopping towards the room but Annie blocks my way. She gives me a huge slap that sends me rolling on the floor:

"Get back there, you little bitch!"

She forces me to accompany her to the front door of the chapel. She knocks on the door. I am still crying. A man opens the door, it is one of the bikers from the other day. I am petrified. He grabs me and pushes me inside:

"Annie entrusts us with her daughter," he says with a laugh, "she's going to sleep with us."

I manage to join the girl of earlier, I embrace her while crying. She looks at me and takes pity on me:

"It's okay, as long as you stay with me nothing will happen to you, just be careful if you see I'm drunk, you stay well behind me."

3. Hostage

In fact, as long as I'm with her, men look at me but don't approach me. But she drinks, and very quickly she is drunk. I hold on and manage to stay against her. Before my childish eyes an orgy is taking place. Women are scarce and naked men are clustered around, I see sexual acts. A link is established in my mind with what I saw Annie doing in bed with Mouloud or when she receives men. I find it hard to look. I cover my eyes. I don't understand everything that is going on, but I am certain that I don't belong there as a child. I hate Annie. Dawn arrives, the activity has diminished but I am still terrified. Many participants are asleep. Nasty smells are rising from the bodies, I think. I stayed snuggled up against my rescuer, almost lying under her, drunk. She threw up, I got some, but I didn't move. Finally, I think no one touched me, but I'm not sure! Slowly, I crawl to the door, a couple is lying in front, I pull on the handle, they grumble but move enough that I manage to crack it open. That's enough. I slip away and run to my house. I lock myself in the bathroom. A few hours later, Annie calls me into the living room, asks me if I had "a good time", I say I did and head for the bedroom. But she follows me and asks specific questions about what I did. I remain vague, I say that I did what I was asked, that people were nice, especially the girl, and also that I danced, like the others. At that moment, I would do anything to get Annie out of the room. In the evening, she calls me to the living room again and hits me. She saw her "friends" and learned that I was not "active":

"You don't know how to have fun, you're not fun, you're ruining my life."

Now, every day, in addition to being beaten, I fear being "forced to caress", that is the term that comes to me to define the particular aggression consisting in being touched by adults in particular places. However, if Annie continues to frolic with her lovers or Mouloud in front of me, there will be no more "experiences" of the chapel type. It must be said that I have little time left to live in Mauguio. Later on, I will wonder if this aspect of my "education" could be a kind of post-Sixties cultural heritage. I read *La familia grande*[8] and I found, for example, points of contact with my experience in the embarrassment of children in front of the nudity, even "neutral" of adults. My shrinks, my friends and my co-author tell me that this is a way of denying a reality that is more horribly clear: I was the victim of my first sexual assault. And it was Annie who organized that assault. My mother.

After that date, she takes a regular lover. I don't like him. "It's Beny," she said one day, as if it was obvious. I will see him again years later, by chance, he will recognize me. He was probably not a bad man.

When Mouloud comes home on weekends, things calm down for me, but they fight with each other. She takes hits and she gives a lot. One day he breaks the TV, another she throws plates against the wall. Once, she throws flaming newspapers in the living room, the fire spreads, they panic, make up while the flames are put out, and then start fighting again. When they are exhausted, Mouloud decides to go and shower. She follows him and stabs him in the arm with a knife. He screams. There is blood everywhere. The neighbors arrive, then the police, called by the neighbors. The police took them both away and we went to sleep at the sisters' house at the school. We stayed there for several days, I think, then one evening, a sister took us home. There is the neighbor and a policewoman. They asked us to pack a small suitcase because we were going to the DDASS. I don't know what it is, but everyone looks very sad.

---

8. *La familia grande*, Camille Kouchner, 2019, Seuil. The book recounts the experience of sexual violence suffered by the author's brother, inflicted by the politician Olivier Duhamel.

It is the end of 1984 or the beginning of 1985. No, it's 1985, because a few days earlier, Grandpa came for Christmas. Usually, nobody comes for Christmas, but this time I am spoiled. Grandpa gave me a wooden house that he had made himself, with little furniture and little dolls inside. I dreamed of it. In the evening, my mother opens her presents and finds a nice leather bag, 68 style. I gently say:

"It is beautiful. When I grow up, I want the same.

His answer hurts me:

- I've waited thirty years to get it, you'll wait at least that long."

Her tone is mean. Maybe she thinks I'm going to steal it from her. She often accuses me of stealing money from her. In reality, she stashes it everywhere, especially in the big drawer in the bathroom and at the bottom of the kitchen dresser. But she forgets. Sometimes she finds it by accident. Last month, I did steal some money from her. I was hungry and my school shoes were completely broken in. I was walking almost barefoot. The shame of doing something wrong was less than the shame of facing my classmates with good shoes.

I gave him a gift. I am very proud of it. It's a book, *Les Misérables*, by Victor Hugo, an illustrated edition. I got it as a prize at school. I like it very much, it's my first prize and I love reading. I give it to her because I value it. She throws it in the trash and says, "This is crap, you didn't pay for it, it's worthless."

The DDASS is an old mansion. My sisters are in one wing and I'm in the other, it's a question of age. I'm happy that my sisters are together, but I have a hard time being separated from them. There are times when I am allowed to see them in the afternoon. Everyday, we get up early, we have breakfast, we clean up. They explain to me that everyone has to participate, but I think that the children participate a lot. I eat so as not to die of hunger, it will take me years to stop eating out of necessity, except when there will be dumplings, or steak purée in my early childhood (the taste will pass me by in Algeria) and, in any case, at the DDASS, there is never any. With my sisters, we went to class in the same building. I love school, but I don't like it. We are too often left alone and the heckling scares me. The classes are mixed but not the dormitories. There were three or four of us per room. After a few weeks, I was sent to a host family. They were nice, but I shut myself off completely. I asked for my sisters. The lady told me that it was impossible for them to be with me. They separate the children, that's the rule. Still today. At the bottom of the garden there is a river. I often go swimming there. It is my only pleasure. For the rest, I mope around. Therefore, I was taken back to the DDASS. The family was nice, but I guess they thought I was really too sad. I am happy to be back with my sisters. Even though we still don't live together most of the time, we are in the same big house.

At night, the rooms are locked. I say that I have to get up often to pee but "it doesn't matter, it's the same for everyone". They give me a bucket for the night. In the morning, when the doors open, I empty my bucket into the toilet and rinse it.

One day, an event that we imagine to be joyful turns into a drama: one of us is going to be placed in a family. For a few days the rumor has been going around, and everyone says that the family is beautiful, rich and big. When the mother and father come to take our friend away, we are all downstairs, except for the one who was to be adopted. An educator goes up to get her. She screams. Our friend has hanged herself. We rush. We see her. But the door is barred to us. They prevent us from entering. I did not see her hanged. The following day, one says to us that she died and we all burst into tears. At the beginning, she seemed to be very happy, it's incomprehensible. She was 15 years old. Some people tried to tell us that she had fainted, that her heart had died... but we know that she hanged herself, even if nobody wants to tell us that she committed suicide. The room she occupied is locked, her two roommates relocated.

I think I discovered at that moment that I want to die, too. I think about it all the time. It will take me years to conceive the idea of suicide, but sometimes, especially after my genitrix hits me, I climb up to the roof and throw my hair, which falls out in handfuls from being pulled. I dream that I am falling with it. It's dying. And then one day, we return to the house in Mauguio, and Annie and Mouloud are there. I don't know what happened to make us feel at home again. I don't have any more memories until the day of departure. That day, the weather is beautiful and we go to the river. I hope they don't get naked. We bathe. I am happy. On the way back, I see Annie packing. She sends me to the room. I feel that something is going to happen. I ask:

"What do we do?

- Shut up, you're leaving, you have your passport in your little bag, you have to be very careful with it.

- Shall I go? Where to? Why do I go? With whom?

- With Mouloud, shut up.

- And my sisters?

- They go too, shut up!"

I say I have to stay. July 14th is coming up, a friend of mine has organized a party, we call it "la boum", I can't miss it! "That's how it is and no other way, and be careful with your papers, don't give them to Mouloud."

Everything goes fast. Without clearly formulating the questions in my head, I ask myself why I should not give my papers to Mouloud. And if my mother is suspicious of Mouloud, why does she allow him to take us away? Everything is in turmoil. I say that my sisters are, but I am not his daughter, why is he taking me away?

I think that at that moment, I don't love anyone anymore, not my parents, not Mouloud, not Grandpa, not Grandma. The DDASS was like a revelation. I am only very afraid for my sisters. I call them "my babies".

Usually when I object like this, Annie hits me, but now she hugs me! It's crazy, this is the first time in my life that she hugs me. That stuns me. They then take advantage of it to load me in the car. The childproof lock is on, I know because I tried to open it, but through the driver's window Annie speaks directly to me:

"You'll be fine, you do everything we tell you."

I don't understand anything, why is she nice? What's going on? Mouloud takes the children's things that Annie hands him, he throws them in the back. We start off. I still resist, I cry, I scream, I hit the front seat. I hope that that is going to attract the neighbors but nobody comes, they are used to it. I end up calming down. At the end of my strength, I fall asleep. I woke up in Marseille, at the port. We boarded a ferry. A customs officer asked for my passport. I say no, I was told not to give it to him. Mouloud insists:

"Give your passport!

- No.

I add:

- He's not my father, I don't want to go with him.

The customs officer pretends not to hear. Mouloud says:

- Look, she's a brat, if you want, I'll call her mother, she'll tell you she has to go with me."

I say that the phone, it will not prove anything... I already know that if they call Annie she will say that I have to leave. I want to sow doubt in the mind of the customs officer. I am not aware that I am being kidnapped. I just don't want to leave. The customs officer finally says:

3. Hostage

"Ah yes, say, she's quite a brat, come by and you can bring me her passport later."

One passes. We park the car. We go towards a cabin. Mouloud tries to catch me, I escape, he catches me. I am afraid he will hit me. He ends up taking my passport away. I cry again. He locks me in the cabin with my sisters. I suppose he goes to see the customs officer. When he comes back, he refuses to give me my passport back. I say I want to call Annie.

"We can't, we're at sea, we'll call him when we get there."

I don't even know where we're going.

4.
All parents are traitors

"The bruises of the soul cannot be seen, but this does not prevent them from being painful. And criminal, for they are indeed inflicted with the purpose of annihilating the other."
Ariane Calvo, *The Psychological Abuse Decoder*,
First ed. 2019.

"The bitch!" I read and reread, detailing the words, but the overall meaning struggles to make its way, through my rage, to my brain. It happened this morning after more than fifteen years of waiting. Mouloud's conviction judgment issued by the Montpellier court on July 30, 1986, for "non-presentation of a child, abduction of a minor without fraud or violence". Let's say that I sometimes searched without searching, let's say that I didn't always want to know, or that I believed that my reconstruction would be better done by a complete detachment from the chaos of my life. And then, last year, more out of habit than out of hope, I contacted the archives department of the Ministry of Justice again, which had told me several times in the past that the judgment had "unfortunately not been digitized in time" or that "the department's move had caused the loss of so many files". And this morning it happened, because it has to happen sometime! In fact, I asked for all the judgments that could concern my "case", without any further details since I still don't know so much about my life! It could concern Mouloud, my mother or my biological father! I started from a certainty - my abduction was "validated" by the French justice system - and from two probabilities, Mouloud had told me several times that he had been in prison because of me, and my biological father had been in prison around 1975. I am still waiting for confirmation of the judgment on the case of my biological father, and even on the fact that Mouloud was physically in prison or not. But the judgment listed in the archives 2529W200 is the first official document that I have received. And it goes against all logic, all my history, all justice since, if it does make Mouloud guilty, it designates as a victim entitled to a compensation of 10,000 francs... my mother!

What anger. In the recitals, I read that Mouloud is guilty "of not having represented, in Mauguio, at the end of July, during August, Fleur and Rose, minor children to Annie V., who had the right to claim them by virtue of an order made on 16-01-1984 by the tribunal de grande instance of Montpellier". Concerning me, my father-in-law is also declared guilty "of having in the same circumstances of time and place, without fraud or violence, kidnapped the young S.[9] minor as being born on 11-07-1974, aged less than 18 years". They even got my date of birth wrong. I was born on August 11! Could anyone use this against me? Now I'm getting paranoid... But there's a reason!" I screamed at the customs officer that it wasn't my father, that I didn't want to leave, that Mouloud forced me to keep quiet, that he coerced and confined me in the cabin... Of course, the court probably didn't

---

9. S. was on my family record book associated with Marie-Claire. I had it removed. Today, I find it difficult to even pronounce it, so much it represents for me the years of the abduction.

know, but then what authorizes them to certify that there was no fraud or violence?

As soon as I read it for the first time, I called Anaïs. It was a relief to share this with her. Anaïs is a criminal lawyer, registered at the bar of Lyon, with a degree in criminology and victimology. She is the association's lawyer and has been invaluable in revising the statutes and clarifying the legal position of ThéraVie ARP-APA anti-RPicide. She was kind and sensitive to my story, of course, but she was not surprised when I told her that Mouloud had taken me away without difficulty: "The problem, you know, is that, even if the law recognizes that the child is discerning from the age of 7, we don't listen to him much." This is why ThéraVie ARP-APA anti-RPicide intends to put the child at the center of the tragedy, and it starts with the imposition of the term "kidnapped" "which has no legal value," Anaïs explains to me, "but it is important to use it so that we understand that the kidnapping of a child does not end when he is found, 'kidnapped' is a status that gives a context and that supposes a psychological and social follow-up, a consideration of the permanence of his suffering in the long term. Yes, kidnapped, I stopped being kidnapped in 1995, "kidnapped", I am forever.

The judgment then specifies that Mouloud did not appear and that it is not certain that he could have been aware of the summons. But the best is for last: in addition to the costs, Mouloud is condemned to pay the sum of 10,000 FF to Annie V., a civil party. Not a word about us, the abducted children. Not a word that suggests an attempt at rescue, not even a thought...

I am not really surprised by Annie's cruel duplicity in placing all the responsibility for the kidnapping on Mouloud. I know, having researched the press archives, that my mother will also contact the association of the Mothers of Algiers, which gathers many mothers of kidnapped children, she, who had her child kidnapped, next to women whose children were kidnapped... I will even discover a photo where she appears next to mothers demanding the release of their children. I am not really surprised but the idea, more or less conscious, that she earned money by having me kidnapped makes me nauseous. So I go and throw up, crying with rage. Then I think back to my arrival in Algiers.

Algiers, summer 1985

It is the beginning of summer. The white city is hot. I look at my sisters, they seem happy, the crossing has amused them. I am 10 years old; even if I can't imagine the ordeal that awaits me, I understand that something disturbing is happening. When we got off the boat, we went to Mouloud's apartment in Telemly, just above the French consulate, but we did not stay there. Let's go to Palm Beach. It is the district of the beautiful coastal residences, many businessmen and politicians live there. The house where we arrive belongs to Mousse, the one from Bangkok. I will discover that they also own a beautiful apartment on Mohamed-V Boulevard... precisely the one where I remember staying with Mouloud after Thailand. I didn't recognize Mousse right away, but I would recognize the apartment, and the link would be made with my previous stay. Still, my childish mind has a hard time determining whether it's good news or bad news that we're at Mousse's place.

There we are, my sisters and I, sitting at a table on the terrace. There is Mouloud, Mousse, his wife, my "aunt" Kima, their children and many "cousins". I know almost nobody. The stone villa is huge and beautiful, there is a swimming pool in front of the terrace, and the gardens lead down to a private beach. On the flat roof of the house, there are pergolas and parasols. I don't know why, but I imagine that we sleep there in the summer. In a corner of the garden, I can see men busy around a brazier, a mechoui is turning on the spit. Mouloud wants to take me for a walk on the beach. I refuse, he insists. I say that I want to take my sisters. He refuses, I insist. I give in. We don't take towels or umbrellas, so we don't go swimming, anyway, it would be inappropriate. I have a hat and my green sandals. As soon as we set foot on the sand, two men come to meet us. I understand that they know Mouloud. One of them stares at me. He horrifies me. He looks like a tramp, with his shaggy hair and his clothes torn in places. With a tone that I find brusque, this man says:

"What the hell are you doing here? I told you never to bring her here again!"

What? Shouldn't I be here? That's good, I want to go too! Mouloud intervenes:

"He's your father."

For me it is the first time that I meet him, I do not make the connection with the man I saw during my first trip. As I look at him, I think of Annie who keeps telling me, "You are crazy like your father." I am afraid he will drive me crazy. I don't want him to touch me. Mouloud insists:

"You know, your dad is my friend."

Maybe he wants to be nice, but it confuses me even more: how did they do their business if they are friends, this man is my father and I live with Mouloud? I stumble and say in a voice so firm that it surprises me:

"I don't care about any of this, I want to go home to France."

My father is calm, he says he loves me and that I am his daughter, but he understands. Why did they arrange this meeting? Is this the

4. All parents are traitors

purpose of our trip? Are we going back to Mauguio now? But then why did they bring my sisters too? It's Mouloud, their father, not this dirty man. We leave my father and return to the house. The méchoui is served. I turn around. My father watches me leave, I try to be natural without having any idea how to be natural in this situation. At the end of the meal, Mouloud and Kima, Mousse's wife, drag me towards the house, I brace myself. *What now?* But I have to follow them, again without my sisters. We go into the hall. Standing by the big mirror, an old woman and a man are waiting for me: my grandmother, "your father's mother," Mouloud says, and my uncle, "his brother. I am very cold. I know what a grandmother and an uncle are. I just don't want them. My grandmother leans towards me but I move away, I refuse to kiss her, she looks like a witch. I say wickedly:

"I don't like you!

- Leave it, Mom," said my uncle, "we're leaving, she's not even our daughter, she's a dirty French girl and a whore like her mother."

I don't know what a whore is but I suspect it's an insult. I answer anyway that I am not dirty. I wash myself every day, and most often at the risk of my life. My grandmother asks her to be quiet.

"That's enough, her mother was 14, my son was 26, it's my son who did the harm, and you see she looks like me, and if we have to we'll do a blood test, but it's our child.

- Yes, we'll do a blood test," my uncle said.

And they leave saying "see you soon". I answer: "No, never. We return to the mechoui.

I look for my sisters. They are playing in the garden.

We stay a long time in this house but I have no idea how long it will take, probably a few weeks. I don't let go of my sisters. I have a feeling that they will be taken away from me. My cousins are numerous and nice. We often go to play on the beach. I live in a kind of worried expectation. Without getting used to it, I adapt, I find my bearings: the beach, the fig tarts that I love, my bed upstairs that is comfortable, Kima, who is nice.

My next memory is Mouloud telling us to get ready because we are going to visit our family in another city. We are going to Annaba. I don't want to go. I think our family is too big. And I am tired of meeting new people. My sisters and I are sitting in Mouloud's gray Mercedes. It's a beautiful car. We go to Hamdane's, Mouloud's brother. This reassures me a little, but I barely have time to calm down when Mouloud explains to me that I must also go to my grandmother's house, the mother of my father from the beach:

"You'll stay the day with them and I'll come back for you." I refuse. He insists. I go there. They live in a residential area by the sea. Perhaps to impress me favorably, Mouloud tells me that they are very rich:

"They also have an apartment in another beautiful area of Annaba, which is a very beautiful city."

I cry when Mouloud drops me off, I want to get back in the car, it's a real crisis. I scream, I stamp my feet. Mouloud and an employee of the house finally get me into the house through the basement. They take me upstairs. My grandmother is there. She tries to calm me down. I drink orangeade and she talks to me a lot. I immediately forget what she says. She shows me a picture of my grandfather who died in 1979. A strange phenomenon takes place in the little girl that I am; I say:

"I once saw this gentleman in a dream when I was little, he was in a bed under the stairs and I gave him an orange and he smiled and ate it and then he went to sleep and never woke up."

I have been dreaming about death since I was 5 years old. At the time, I told my mother about this dream and she didn't care, but my grandmother said:

"Your grandfather died like this, it was your cousin who gave him the orange, and then he fell asleep, the next day he died."

I am still shocked. Later, I will research psychogenealogy and especially the disturbing phenomena of "birthday syndrome" or "invisible family loyalties[10] ", but for now I have the retrospective fear of my dream. And above all, I tell myself that it must be my real family since I had this dream.

Things start to fall into place in my head. I understand that the dirty man I saw on the beach and the one I had seen once in Telemly, and that I had been introduced as a friend of Mouloud, are the same person, my father. Decidedly, everyone lies to me.

We enter a large living room where people are gathered. The whole family is there, and the fact that they have come to meet me adds to my terror. You don't move a whole family for a child's tea party. It's an event. I am the event. There are cakes, mint water; I feel like a doll being carried around. I'll really understand it later, but I can already sense that they are happy, like when you celebrate a victory. But at this point, I still think I'm going back to France very soon. Everyone speaks French to address me but they speak Arabic to each other. It bothers me a lot.

Yemma introduces me to Noury, another uncle. Noury speaks up and addresses me directly, everyone hears:

"I am your tutor, I will raise you, your name is S., you are a Muslim...

I shout. He raises his voice:

- Don't look at me like that. Here, children and women do not answer when men speak.

I answer in a nutshell:

---

10. Unconscious repetitions of acts, diseases, traumas, through several generations. Anne Ancelin Schützenberger, professor of psychology at the University of Nice, is the leading specialist in psychogenealogy.

- I am not a Muslim and I have the right to speak.

- You are the daughter of a Muslim so you are a Muslim.

I yell:

- Fuck you!

 I know what it means, Annie has told me enough. Heavy silence.

- It's very rude, you'll regret it.

My grandmother interjects:

- That's enough."

Crying, I explain that I am waiting for Mouloud who promised to return. Around me people whisper. I have the feeling of a trap. Obviously, Mouloud does not come. The night falls. I refuse to eat, I cry all the time. My grandmother tells me that I will sleep with her. We go to her room. I refuse to lie down. I am afraid not to wake up. I sit on the couch like someone who is waiting. I realize that I don't know who to call. Where to reach Mouloud? Or Annie? I don't have the phone numbers, or even the exact addresses, and I don't know where to go. When I wake up, I tell my grandmother that I have to call Mouloud:

"I have to go home.

Yemma looks at me with a mixture of decision and tenderness, then says the words that will resonate in me forever:

- This is your home now."

5.
The trap is closing

"The passion for truth and justice cannot, without questioning itself, accept such a deception."
Frantz Fanon, "L'Algérie face aux tortionnaires français",
El Moudjahid n° 10, 1957.

"No, but I'm not going to do a book about my mother!" Here I am arguing with my co-author. He thinks I'm not clear with her. A mother is not simple for anyone, but mine is as good as any Medea in hell. For as long as I can remember, I have been aware that I was an unwanted child. But from unwanted to beaten, delivered to men, starved or kidnapped, there is a margin, isn't there? As a child refused from the beginning of her pregnancy, I was hated as Annie's failures went on, until I became the symbol and the cause of her failed life. Besides, did she really refuse me? It takes a will, a conscience to refuse! She rather forgot me, hoping perhaps that a providential Holy Spirit of the gourds would free her from her tumor like a ripe scab falls from a knee... Conceived undoubtedly in some pitiful biological emergency, I was going to disappear as I had come, by chance! Of course, she had heard about the angel makers in Lons or Dijon, but wasn't she risking hell? And where to find the money? And what's the point! And time goes by... I am the child of chance and its foolishness... and of the absence of effective contraception!

I never call her "my mother", but during the hardest part of my Algerian ordeal, she is still the figure of hope for me. It is to her that I dream of returning, to Mauguio. Am I crazy? Maybe, but it's still not enough. Why do we do this? For the last forty years or so that I've been thinking about it, I think I've found a clue: I had no choice. What I was enduring with Noury was so violent that I needed a dose of imaginary love at least equal to that of the violence of the situation to endure it. And if I didn't have this compensating dose, I had to invent it. To invent the love of a mother for the time necessary for my survival. I didn't think about it, I didn't "think" this method of survival, it was imposed on me. My mother had to be the mental buoy that would ensure my survival because I had no other. Isn't that what my revenge is all about? Could Annie's hatred have filled this role? Perhaps, but to the 10 year old child that I was, love seemed simpler, more secure. So the idealization of the mother figure served as my lifeline. I had to love my mother in order not to die in hell. I still remember the face of the first shrink to whom I told this... Generally speaking, during those terrible years, I will have the pleasure, for hours on end, of replaying in my head, like a balm on my pain, the beautiful things of France and the beautiful moments spent with my aunts Irine or Alice.

On the other hand, I believe that there is a close connection between my epilepsy, my long COVID, my ankylosing spondylitis, and the certainty anchored in the depths of my soul that I don't belong anywhere, because at the beginning of my life I was not wanted. I sometimes say to my *sister* Marine that I am the sick muse of Baudelaire and that one would see "reflected on (my) complexion, madness and horror, cold and taciturn". "It's seriously relou", she usually replies. Recently, I learned that in addition to immutable genes, we pass on to our children mutated alleles and nucleotide sequences... which are directly dependent on influences, the context of upbringing, and that the receiving individual will be affected positively or negatively depending on whether he or she has received a lot of love or a lot of whipping. This is called epigenetics[11], it is an experimental science " and it is shit, you see, because I, love..."

Not having been wanted put me in danger biologically.

When I will learn, in 1996, that I am expecting Laure, my first decision, beyond any rationality, will be to rush to a psychologist of association to ask the only question which knots my guts: *Will I be a bad mother?Do we inevitably reproduce what we have experienced? Will I beat my child because I was beaten?* The answer is complex, as we know, but to this day I have never laid a hand on my daughter and at no time in her life has she stopped being the heart of mine.

It is his role, my co-author's, to bring an outside look that can search the hollows of my soul and the voids of my life. Me, I am much too close! He is right, my mother is a central character in my story. She is even the one around whom the pain of my life, my game with death and all my hate are organized.

But damn, we're not going to make a book about my mother!

After all, her denial of my existence frees me from my debt of nature. If nobody gave me life, and first of all not Annie, then I owe nothing to anybody, and first of all not to Annie.

So I can look forward to his death.

---

11. Discipline of biology that studies the nature of mechanisms that reversibly, transmissibly and adaptively modify gene expression without changing the nucleotide sequence. In other words, what is transmitted in the DNA that is not immutable, acquired.

Annaba, summer 1985[12]

I look at my grandmother with sadness:

"But no, my home is in France, with my sisters and my mother; I don't know you and I don't want to know you.

My "you" includes all the people I have been introduced to since I arrived in Algeria. She looks away:

- It's us, your family, it's Noury your guardian."

I am completely panicked. At breakfast, I refuse to eat. Noury is present, he is the one who speaks:

"You are Algerian, Muslim, you have to live in your father's country and in his house, you are going to stay here and you better accept it right away.

- But Mouloud..., I said.

- Mouloud is your stepfather, he cheated on your real father. And both of them explain to me what adultery is and how my mother committed it!

"When he got home, they were in bed," adds Noury, "and your father caught them there, he's a slut!"

In bed, then. And if Annie is a slut, it is quite logical that I am a slut too. Yemma insists:

"Your mother and Mouloud are horrible, they hit you, we know it, they are bad for you."

I would like to object that Mouloud does not hit me regularly, even though he is impulsive and brutal, but I have already understood that this will have no effect.

A thousand questions are assailing me and I still feel torn, because it is true that my life is hard in Mauguio. Will it be better here? Will

---

12. Like one of the characters in François Ozon's beautiful film (L'été 85), my destiny is mortifying.

they stop strangling me? And how will I go to school? And I understand that my "new family" speaks French, but everyone outside speaks Arabic: how will I make myself understood? How will I make new friends? No, no and no! I don't want to stay here. And even if my new family loves me, there will always be in my head the idea that I have been cheated, that I have been stolen, literally, I have been stolen from my family, as rotten as it is, from my village, my country, my history! What are we building on this? How am I going to grow up with this? The first question still occupies me today. The second, on the other hand, was settled right away: I stopped growing as soon as I was kidnapped. A few days later, but I don't know how long it took, Mouloud returned. He knocks on the door, I am happy he is there, but they push him away, he screams. I understand that he is drunk, as he often is. Through the moucharabiehs of the hall, I see him staggering back to his car. I feel a little ashamed. He sits behind the wheel, then sticks his head out - the roof of Mouloud's Mercedes can open!- and shouts, "Give me back my daughter, I love her, I will marry her and she will take care of her sisters."

Marry me? My sisters! I see them, they are sitting at the back, I run to the door, Yemma holds me back, I kick, she screams, Noury takes me under the arm and throws me back. My grandmother grabs the phone and calls the police. Half an hour later, while I am still in the hall, guarded by Yemma, the police arrive and send Mouloud away. They don't arrest him, even though he is drunk.

My next memory is the beginning of the school year. I still think I'm going back to France, I keep telling my grandmother that I have my things, my friends, my school there... But Yemma explains to me that from now on my life is in Algeria and not in France. I insist, and even :

"I might come back to see you for the vacations."

5. The trap is closing

No, I will go to the French school Pierre and Marie Curie in Annaba and that's it.

And then one morning in September, Annie came. This memory was only "reformulated" with precision in my memory in 2020, during a psych session. But it is now clear: I hear her voice in the hall, I run down the stairs and... in a fraction of a second and a look of contempt, she makes me go from the certainty of returning to France to the certainty of staying there forever, from confidence to distress. But that doesn't stop me, I have to go back. I run to her and want to kiss her. Her hands reach out, but it is to keep me at a distance. His gesture is unforgettable. Without hardness, he tells me no in one block, immutably no, no to what I am, no to my future, no to any hope. No.

She locks herself in with Yemma and Noury. For a long time, I think. Then she goes up to see me in my room:

"You are going to live here now, they bought you. You're being punished, you shouldn't have told the police, the DDASS... everything that happens at home.

I cry. She is on the doorstep, she looks at me one last time:

- You're going to take a lot of heat for this and it's good for you, it's your fault."

I don't know if they "bought" me, if Yemma gave money to Annie, I was never told about it again. It is not impossible, the family is rich. It belongs to this caste close to the power, which, after the war, was deliciously cast in the clothes of the dominant colonial. She is the Algerian bourgeoisie fought by Frantz Fanon, the one that replaced the colonial bourgeoisie fought by Albert Camus. And, from this point of view at least, independence has changed everything so that nothing ever changes.

But why is it my fault? I'll be thinking about it for forty years.

After Annie's departure, I cry a lot, but I remember that I can't scream. I'm devastated, stunned.

Sold, given away, and even kidnapped... At that moment, I can't put into words what is happening to me. It would take me years to understand that Annie was, at the very least, an accomplice to the kidnapping. Even today, if the childhood part of me no longer rejects the guilt of her parents - how can I do that, reasonably? -I often try to understand them in their defense.

When I was there, it was impossible, physically impossible, it would even have been counterproductive, the shrinks explained to me that it would have provoked a psychological collapse. So I made of Annie this idealized island of sincerity and trust, evacuating everything that could obscure this vision, and obviously her violent behavior, her dislike, her excesses. What an irony, Annie became my mother after she had me kidnapped.

Often, Yemma and Noury tell me that Algeria is my country, I answer that it is my father's, but not my mother's, nor mine. I answer that it is my father's, but not my mother's, nor mine. "I was born in France", I will repeat to them over and over again as soon as I discover that it annoys them deeply.

The school year started. I was enrolled in the Pierre and Marie Curie class, but very quickly, a few weeks after the start of classes, Noury announced that I would be going to another school. It was a punishment because of my behavior, I cried all the time, I didn't want to do what Noury said, I locked myself in my room, I said bad words... In my new school, nobody spoke French. And I don't understand anything, obviously, so they put me in CP when I should be in CM2. As I am also tall for my age, people look at me, make fun of me, I am "the French girl sitting at the back", "the one who doesn't understand anything". The children speak Arabic

5. The trap is closing

among themselves, and when they speak French it is often to mock or insult me. I hate this language. I hate them. Fortunately, one day a teacher came to see Yemma and they ended up putting me in a bilingual class. I started to work well, especially when it was in French. I also learned Arabic, but I refused to show it to Yemma or Noury. One day, I came home with a zero on a science exam in Arabic; usually, the questions were in both languages, but there it was just in Arabic. When Noury came to pick me up (usually it was a cousin or a driver who came, anyway I never go out alone), he asked me for my grade, I said: "I have two fried eggs!", showing my double zero on my copy. He slaps me very hard in front of everyone, shouting that I must respect the school, that I must respect him, my tutor! I defend myself by saying that I don't understand anything, that it was in Arabic... I ask to go back to the French school, I take one more.

Why did Noury become my guardian? First, because my biological father is deficient. His brothers and Yemma say he is crazy. They had him committed and will often change him from one institution to another.

When he obtained this official administrative status which gave him the responsibility of my education and, in practice, the right of life and death over me, Noury was 23 years old. From the height of my 10 years, I see him as "a grown-up" but, with the years, I will wonder. I will even ask Yemma the question:

"Why is Noury my tutor? Why isn't it you? Or Moufid, Azz or another brother?

- It has to be a man, that's the Algerian law," Yemma answers me, "and Noury was the only one single at that time.

That's not true, Moufid, the lawyer, was not married either. I believe that Yemma chose Noury because she thought it would be easier to impose her authority on her, the "mother", Yemma. I also believe that she realized her mistake quite quickly, but it was too late.

Noury is a young adult, he is also studying, he is finishing his degree in petrochemical engineering and preparing his defense. Everyone says that he is smart and that he has a great future in science. When he defended his thesis the following year, he received the best grade and was awarded a scholarship to continue his studies in New York.

But (his) Allah did not want it to be so.

6.
In the madness of fundamentalism

"You have to go through the night: strip yourself of all external attributes, and endure the anguish."
Claire Marin, *Rupture(s),* Éd. de l'Observatoire, 2019.

I live with death. I have wished it for a long time. Does it take courage to die? Today, this is one of the subjects I frequently discuss with my therapist. I always thought I would die, when I was a child, because of Annie's blows, then Noury's, the Islamists', the police's, then the ulcer's, the COVID's... And then not. Today I believe that I will never commit suicide. Because there is Laure. For Laure, and the wonderful love she puts in my life. And then there is life, and it is strong, stronger than adversity no doubt... In Algeria, on the other hand, I often resolved to die. Without actually doing it. I think that if I had stayed I would have died anyway. Suicide or not. For me, death is latent and defeatist, its presence does not create the urgency to live, which I feel deep inside. It appears rather like a headache, then goes away. Accepting and understanding myself is an ongoing process. One day, in Italy, I saw a sentence on a wall: *Il silenzio uccide più della mafia,* "silence kills more than the mafia". This is what happened to me. Silence almost killed me so many times.

I am also an expert in pain and suffering... that has been my subject for forty-eight years. Black belt. This morning, while I've been trying for twenty minutes to unfold my left arm, I listen to the philosopher Claire Marin talk about the subject on the radio. When one is unfamiliar with the notion, that is, when the experience of pain covers a spectrum that goes from toothache to the fantasized suffering of young Werther, one easily confuses the two. I don't. Basically, pain is physical, it is a doctor's vocabulary. It is, says the WHO, "an unpleasant sensory and emotional experience".

The suffering, it, would be the product of the pain, what one feels after, on the duration. The pain is punctual, acute, temporary, registered in the present, immobile; the suffering is vital and sentimental. It is also the opinion of Montaigne, for whom the pain is often only the conscience that one has of it. Consciousness that a strong and reasoned spirit will naturally be able to control. Montaigne had heartaches and kidney stones, that hurts but nobody ever buried him alive.

For Marguerite Duras, it is false. The author of *La Douleur* inscribes her concept in the duration, so much so that she names "pain" the recomposition, after the war, of the memories of her deported husband, from his daily journal. It is thus a construction which exceeds the affect, it is an artifice mobilizing the entirety of the subject, which constitutes its pain...

I believe that pain leads to suffering, but that continuous suffering constitutes, at the seam of the soul and the body, a new and ungovernable pain, because it abolishes time.

For me, the remedy to the immediate experience of pain has often been to step outside my body to observe it in its torment. In cognitive psychology, it is explained by a failure of transmission of tactile and visual proprioceptive information of the body, a field which covers the synaptic connections relating to the perception of one's body by the muscles and the articulations. The phenomenon is even biologically localized: it is located at the temporo-parietal junction. A sudden and violent activation of this area of the brain can then cause the creation of a virtual replica of oneself outside the body. The point of view on oneself is shifted and the vision is "demarcated" from the bodily perception, until it provides a figurative perception. For a long time, we were satisfied with spiritualist, religious or esoteric explanations of the phenomenon, but Charles Tart[13] , an American psychologist, set up the first quantitative study on the subject in the 1960s. Conclusion: the phenomenon has three causes of triggering, drugs, hypnosis and extreme fear.

I had my share of fear. The first time I felt this strange detachment was in France, every time Annie strangled me; then on the train with Mouloud when the police stopped us; when the policeman broke my disc of Maya the Bee on my head; not when I witnessed the scene in the chapel, it's strange, it's the emptiness; but it started again when Annie stabbed me. And then in Algeria, so many times...

Annaba, summer 1985

Without ever agreeing to anything and while constantly asking Noury and Yemma to be able to go back to France, I must admit that the first months of my life in Algeria were not so bad. Yemma often takes me to the beach or for a walk on the seafront. Every Saturday I go to the movies with Noury and his friends; sometimes my cousin Raf is there too. We see a lot of horror movies, *Return of the Living*

---

13. Charles T. Tart (born in 1937), American psychologist specializing in altered states of consciousness, he is the father of transpersonal psychology.

6. In the madness of fundamentalism

Dead, Friday the 13th, but others, too; even today, I see *Out of Africa* every year, which I saw there for the first time. We also go to restaurants on the Corniche, I discover Algerian cuisine, which I love, *mechwi*, couscous, *bourek*... Even today, I cook my own *chekchouka*, a delicious mixture of tomatoes, peppers, onions and fresh eggs that I season with fresh coriander and cumin. Laure loves it too.

It's a life that could be a bit like France, but better, because Annie never took me to restaurants or movies. The winter is more difficult. This is my first winter in Algeria. In addition to the kidnapping and the conviction of being a prisoner, I wasted away physically. I had my first allergies; I couldn't stand the humidity and it rained all the time. From the summer of 1986, the situation degenerated radically... Noury became more and more nasty. He often mentions Islam. I don't understand much, but I am afraid when he talks about it. And one day I overheard a conversation in French with his brother: "No way, I won't go to study with those miscreants", Noury told Moufid who asked him if he was going to accept the proposal of the University of New York. This is my first concrete memory of Noury's radicalization. He chose to stay in Annaba, where he immediately obtained a position at the national research laboratory in physics and chemistry. It's a bit like entering the CNRS at the age of 24 through the front door! This is exceptional and obviously due to his exit rank, but we will know later in the family that this consecration was greatly made possible by Noury's connections with powerful networks, notably among the Islamists of the region. His commitment stipulates that a certain number of hours be devoted to teaching at the local high school. He therefore took on the position of physics and chemistry teacher in a high school in Annaba, but he soon refused to work for Algeria: "This government is also made up of miscreants. He often says that it is necessary "to bring back Islam to the heart of the university". His brothers and, above all, his mother Yemma disapprove of him, but do not oppose him head-on. Without anything ever being formulated - at least at the beginning - everyone knows that Noury's "friends" are powerful and dangerous. Little by little, he acquires a kind of ascendancy. He establishes his power over the whole family. And first of all over me.

At the end of the summer, I also learned that I had to wear a veil. I was 12 years old.

"She has reached puberty, she must submit to the law of Allah," Noury argues in Yemma's presence. In fact, I've been in puberty for a year now, but I haven't told anyone. Last week, he found out. Yemma tries to object:

"It can wait, she'll veil when she's old like me, or a widow!"

The veil of old age is more cultural than religious, the stake of submission to the man is also less attached to it because the woman, by her age or her widowhood, is supposed to have acquired a kind of prestige or respectability, it is a scarf. In my case, I have to wear the veil because Islam demands it! And especially Noury. The period that opens in the summer of 1986 is really horrible. As a tutor, Noury alone has the legal authority[14] . But, in a general way, he now has authority

---

14. I don't know the details of my "adoption". In Koranic law, which applies in Algeria, full adoption is forbidden, only *kafala* is possible. It is a religious adoption that does not entail a filiation link and excludes the adopted person from the name of the adopter - and from any transmission, obviously. The *kafala* can be notarial or judicial. I believe that the judicial act, in my case, has not been completed because I will learn in 2019 that my Algerian "citizenship" does not meet all the criteria. However, a legal guardian is appointed in all cases. In theory, this guardianship ceases when the adoptee reaches the age of majority, 18 years in my case (the age of majority in Algeria will be raised to 19 years in 2014). I was obviously unaware of this but, in fact, without papers or status, I am a prisoner before and after my majority. N.B.: with other modalities, the *kafala* is also the system that has allowed, for years, the slave exploitation of foreign workers in Qatar before the 2022 soccer world cup. Like me, the slaves in Qatar were also forbidden to leave the country without the permission of their "guardian".

6. In the madness of fundamentalism

over the family, he takes charge of the management of the accounts and the household staff, and commands everyone. And I become - I realize it quite quickly - an instrument of his power. He knows that Yemma has taken an affection for me that is often cowardly but sometimes sincere, and he will play on it. His brothers do not hate me either. I am rather indifferent to them. They each have their own life and have little time for me.

At that time, while the idea of a new and anxious school year was already in my mind, I decided to escape. One afternoon, the opportunity arose. The neighbor's children are playing hoop in the street in front of our house, and I ask Yemma if I can join them. Noury is not there, she agrees. I join my friends, under the surveillance of one of Noury's drivers, who stays in front of our gate. I know my little friends well but I don't often play with them because I am rarely allowed to go out. They celebrate me, they like me, I am "the French girl". A few meters away, their parents are having tea in the garden. I brought my own hoop so I could walk away quietly, so I threw it far enough and ran after it. At the corner, I turn around: the guard hasn't seen me, nor have my friends' parents. A little cousin looks at me. I think he understands. I abandon the hoop and start running down the perpendicular street. I have a plan. From my experience living in France, I have learned a lesson in the face of danger: I must take shelter under the protection of an authority greater than my family. Two words come to mind: police and court. I have experience with both. As the signs are bilingual and we are close to the center of Annaba, I quickly find a "police station", I wait to discover a "court" to have the choice... Here it is! I choose the court because of the memory of my Maya the bee disc broken in two by a policeman. I enter the building and tell the guard that "I want to see someone in an emergency office". He laughs. I cry, I beg, I scream. He takes me to an office. I wait a long time. I think I am going to see a judge in a suit, a lawyer, or a policeman.

The door opens. It's Noury. He is friendly but I know that when we get home he will hit me. End of the story.

After this story, my relationship with my grandmother cooled down considerably. She was convinced that I had to be controlled, or at least punished. Noury forces me to wear the veil permanently. Normally, it can be removed at home when there are only girls, but I have more cousins than a character in a book by Alice Zeniter, so I am veiled from morning to night.

Noury takes me to the mosque every morning. The preaching I attend is in French. But before I leave, I have to clean the floor where I live. This is a rule that I have learned, with a lot of hard work, not to evade because my tutor meticulously checks the cupboards and beds after the execution. I get up at dawn. In France, I read a children's version of Les *Misérables*. I feel like Cosette. I am a veiled Cosette.

August 11, it is my birthday. I have not been told anything but I see that the driver and the cook are busy. A party is being prepared. I am on my guard but still happy. I interpret it as an improvement of my condition, a small return to grace, a sign that things are getting better... A huge cake, a mountain at least one meter high, is enthroned in the middle of the living room. Guests arrive. During the day, I am dressed in different traditional costumes. My hands are made with henna. I have to dance. I am wearing the *"quatifa"* dress, burgundy velvet embroidered with gold thread. It is explained to me that the belt carries very expensive jewels, ancestral. All this is surely very expensive, hundreds of thousands of euros perhaps but I do not know. Several times, I meet the eyes of a man. He stares at me. This worries me. From the beginning of the afternoon, I start to hate this party. I am sure that they are hiding something from me. Later,

6. In the madness of fundamentalism

when I'm 16, I'll understand that this party was about my promise to a man. He's there, but I don't know it. In fact, I think it's my birthday. But I was promised to Abdel X., a French-Algerian; he is the son of a French convert, Genny, who came, I think, from Normandy. He has done several training courses in Afghanistan.

At the beginning of the 1986 school year, I continued to go to the mosque but, in order to make my religious practice compatible with school classes, I now attended the evening preaching. I never wanted to go, I was dragged there violently. Little by little, Noury forbids me music and TV; I don't miss Algerian TV. As for the veil, my cousins are always there, so I never take it off. Sometimes I take it off in a fit of anger, then Noury beats me. I still do the cleaning in the morning before school. I understand that it is a punishment because they are rich and there are servants. I am fully aware that they want to humiliate me, to tear me to pieces.

At school, on the other hand, things are going well. At the end of the year, in June 1987, I even got the first Francophonie prize. This was perhaps to encourage me because I was progressing in all subjects, especially when the teaching was in French, but my level of Arabic was improving a lot, even if I still refused to speak it with Noury and Yemma. All the parents are invited to the award ceremony. I am proud and happy. Noury comes because Yemma insists, but reluctantly. He is badly dressed, with his gandoura from home and his blue flip-flops. I think he doesn't like the fact that I am honored. He should be happy though, since he keeps telling me to work well and to show respect for my teachers, the school, Algeria, God... It's my turn, I'm going to be called to the stage, Noury takes my arm:

"You are a Muslim, you must not touch anyone, it is sinful, you take the gift and that's it."

These are only words, I am used to blows, to violence, but these words hurt me a lot. They paralyze me in a moment of joy. I decide to face it:

"That's not very polite what you're asking me."

His gaze is bloody. I am called, I walk in the middle of the alley and I forget everything, the looks of my comrades make me feel good. Of course there will be some who will mock "the French girl", who will be jealous of her... but this is my moment. Whatever my life, whatever the circumstances that brought me here, I am proud. The director hands me a book, leans over and kisses me. I ostensibly give in. I smile. I know the punishment will be violent, but I want this moment when the world is stopped to fill my soul and my body. The director says a few words that I forget, but I remember the word "example," and then I walk back down the stage and to my seat. Before I sit down, my uncle stands up and slaps me. I fall to the floor. I hear a clamor around me. I am stunned. *My book!* The director approaches and speaks to Noury, but it is Noury who raises his voice. The director returns to the stage and the ceremony continues. I clutch my book and cry inside.

A few weeks later, my first Ramadan arrived. My grandmother doesn't agree but Noury insists. So Yemma hid some food in her room and told me I could go if I was hungry but I had to wait until Noury was out of the house. But Noury catches me the first time I go to eat. He unbuckles his belt and I understand that this is going to be terrible. He turns me over and whips me on my feet and legs and buttocks. My grandmother arrives shouting:

"She has her rules, she has her rules, she has the right!

Noury stops, puts his belt back on and says:

- She will have to make up the days."

I'm in a lot of pain.

7.
The raped child

"Our bodies are the texts that carry the memories."
Bessel van der Kolk, *The body forgets nothing*, Albin Michel, 2014.

"I can talk to you for hours about the beatings, the hunger, the torture or Annie's betrayal, but this is fucking hard. I am with Olivier at the terrace of the Barlu, quai de Seine. I like the terraces of Paris in springtime, pulling up a chair and "watching France go by" as in a nice song by Gauvain Sers. Except that Olivier and I are working. We even wrote half the book on the Ourcq canal! It bothers me because it touches the deepest part of my being and that, forty years later, I have no idea of the extent of the damage. I have no idea of the extent of the damage because I have never spoken about it, or almost never, or never really spoken about it! I remember a very touching intervention by Corinne Masiero on Sonia Devillers' microphone[15] . She speaks in her own language, so powerful and delicate, of her experience of incest, of her long silence, then of forgetting, or rather of a form of traumatic amnesia that refuses the reality of violence, then of

---

15. The guest of " La Matinale ", Sonia Devillers, Sept. 19, 2022. Corinne Masiero comes back on the testimony she gives to Andréa Rawlins-Gaston for the film *Incest, say it and hear it*, broadcast on France 3, Sept. 26, 2022.

the urgency to speak about it after the shock felt, by chance, when finding the photo of an aggressor. I too have buried. I too remember the blows in the face much better than the horrible caresses. But I too have photos...

"We don't have to talk about it at all, we can forget about it if you want," my co-author offers.

- Well, no, we never forget, never. So maybe the things we will never forget, it's better to learn to live with them, right?

- Yes, perhaps.

- Well, imagine..."

I am 12 years old, I have been abducted for a little over a year. I have been in bed for a few minutes. Like every night, I oscillate between tears and France... that is to say, I look for beautiful thoughts from my past to fall asleep. Mostly, I think about the river at the bottom of the garden, about my aunts Irine and Alice's Christmas presents or about Mémé's pancakes. I avoid thinking about my sisters, even though they come back all the time. Throughout my captivity, I will make them small gifts, poems, small jewels, sewn clothes... that I will hide in the hope of giving them one day. Noury enters my room without making a sound. I am immediately suspicious because he doesn't look angry. And he doesn't usually enter quietly. He has a funny look. He comes closer.

From the beginning, in the summer of 1985, I hated its touch. It is slimy and dangerous, like a honey cake with thorns. I hate honey. Between the blows, he often has moments of false gentleness, attempts to approach, hugs, caresses... I am suspicious, of course, but without emotional reference, without "experience", I thought "he was trying to be nice" or "we do that to children".

My ridiculous escape attempt last month is not forgotten in the family, my freedom perimeter remains very limited. I go to school with a driver. He comes back to pick me up. I don't play in the street anymore, but in the garden, here or when we go to the beach house, I am sometimes left alone. I would like to read books in French, but there are none. And I am not allowed to go into town. I have eczema on my forehead and I'm happy to finally take it off. My moments of respite are in the evening, after Noury leaves, because I am alone. My grandmother is an enigma. Sometimes I understand that she is trying to protect me, and even to save me from some of Noury's blows, but when I am beaten, most of the time she does not react. She does not oppose Noury; yet he is her son, she could tell him not to hit me, couldn't she? She says she loves me and that I have to do well in school. Sometimes she talks to me about Annie. Noury too, but it is to tell me that she is a French whore, and often that I am too. Yemma says that my mother can come to see me whenever she wants, she is not prevented, but it is she who does not want to come. I know that this is plausible but I say that it is not true.

That evening, Noury has a strange air. Almost kind. This is not good at all. He sits at the foot of my bed:

"I am your guardian, you know, it's my job to protect you from the outside world and the miscreants. Everything I do is for your own good.

- I know, yes, I whisper, pulling up the blanket a bit.

- And since I know you have nightmares at night, I came to sleep with you so that you would be more peaceful.

I am petrified.

- Thank you, tonight is fine, I was about to fall asleep."

He says nothing and lies down on the bed. He takes me in his arms from behind. I feel his beard on my neck and his breath.

"It's okay, I say, tonight is okay..."

He gets under the blanket.

"No, but really it's okay."

His hand is on my legs in front. I'm afraid to pee. My brain doesn't work anymore, as if I was on pause, in a kind of infinite waiting. Even now I can't remember any details, except that he pulls me back and starts rubbing against me. Gently? Violently? How long? I have no idea, but the words still resonate in me:

"You are the devil, you know you are the devil."

My God, the devil! Without doubt he caresses me, he will do it later, without doubt I try to escape, without doubt he takes me back. My memory becomes again more assured: he pushes me back violently to look at me in the eyes. I want to look elsewhere, not to see him, *please...* He straightens me and tightens me to the shoulders.

"Temptress, you are a temptress."

He leaves the room in a rage, after slapping me. It will take me months to intellectually integrate what happened. My pajama pants are all greasy. I don't know what a temptress is. I imagine it must be close to a French whore. I'm afraid he'll come back. I don't fall asleep until the morning. The next night he comes back to tuck me in and he touches me again. He starts spending more and more time in my room. He calls it "looking after me". He rubs me. A little later in the winter, he starts stroking me in front. Why does one image rather than another become imprinted on a brain for life? For me, it is not the one of intrusions, of violence; surprisingly, the image that will never fade from my memory, the one that sometimes comes back unexpectedly at the terrace of a café or in the middle of the night, it is the one, stinking and so physical, of Noury putting back his underwear.

"That evening in the summer of 1986 was the first time. It will happen again whenever he decides, which is almost every day from the time I was 12 until I was 20."

It's summer and it's hot on the Ourcq canal, but I shiver.

Annaba, summer 1986

From time to time, my biological father comes to visit the family. They explain to me that it's a kind of "leave", like for the soldiers. But I was never told, and it was often on a school day. One day, he arrived during lunch, probably on a Sunday. He was very upset, he shouted:

"My brother is in love with my daughter, this has to stop.

My grandmother bows her head, she says:

- Yes, Noury, this must stop.

- I look after her, it is my role since you are unable to do so," says Noury.

I don't know what my father answers, Yemma makes me leave. I don't have the words anyway. After this revelation in front of everyone, Noury takes me to the garden, he beats me, I can't walk for several days. My face is huge, I can't turn my head...

I am 15 years old. I am getting sick more and more often. Moufid, another of Noury's brothers, took out health insurance for me and I went to see several doctors. They give me vaccinations. My legs and knees often hurt and I lose my balance. I fell down the stairs in my room and hurt myself. It was Noura, Noury's wife, who found me. I don't like her. She and Noury got married in late 1990. One day, at the mosque, we met his future wife and he introduced me to her. I know that it is not a coincidence. I don't know why he does this. As if my opinion counted.

When Noura picks me up, I can't stand up:

"You still want to do your interesting!"

But as soon as she lets go of me I fall again and there they understand that something serious has happened. I think it's because of the evening, when Noury rubs herself. Maybe I am pregnant.

At the last doctor's, the strongest, Yemma accompanies me. His office is in the hospital. I stay all day. I do a lot of tests of all kinds with wires connected to me. At the end of the day, I have RAA, Rheumatic fever. It's a kind of paralysis, not serious but still serious. They tell me it's because of a "strep throat". I burn to ask if it could be from Noury's rubbing, I don't dare, but for years, without having any idea of the shape or consistency of this "creature", I will associate Noury with a "streptococcus", it will help me. It is a type A streptococcus, there are many different types. You can see it because you measure it with the "ASLO", something, an enzyme I think, that you must have in your body, but you can't have more than two hundred, I have eight hundred. Every two weeks for five years, I will have to get an injection. On the box of the injection, it is written: 1.5 million units of penicillin. At first, a nurse comes to my home, but when I faint, she says it's too much responsibility for her and we have to go back to the hospital. Every day I also have to take a pill at home, but I often throw it up and get a stomach ulcer. We went back to the hospital. I have a 2 mm perforation. I have to take Tagamet and Natisedine[16] , this is the treatment for the ulcer. And I'm becoming allergic to a lot of things, starting with pollens. I get colds all the time. The allergies will cause asthma. I need to be "desensitized". The asthma stops. I also take Tranxene. I don't know that it's an anxiolytic. I fall asleep all the time. At school, I was so dazed that a few weeks later, I fell down during a French class. The director asked me if I was taking drugs! This reminds me of Mauguio and Annie! I made the connection with Tranxene. I decide not to say anything but I stop the treatment. The idea comes to me that they also want to fill me with drugs to put me in an asylum like dad.

I keep asking my grandmother if I can go back to Mauguio to Annie's house. I propose again to live in both countries... "I will come to see you on vacations!" My grandmother replies that she would

---

16. This drug, very dangerous for the neurological system, is now prohibited.

like to but that "it is Noury who decides". Almost every day we watch videos from Afghanistan with Noury. There are men on horseback, a mujahid soldier all surrounded by white. They shoot him, he falls and dies, and his face lights up because he is going to heaven. One day, there is a demonstration near us. Noury's friends won the elections[17] but they were cancelled[18] . Noury wants to take me to the demonstration. I don't want to go. Yemma and Moufid tell him that it is not my place. Noury says that his brothers are all miscreants, especially Azz, who just married a strange girl.

One day, Yemma said to Noury:

"So you wish your brothers dead too?

- Yes, and from you too, because you are a miscreant."

It is at this time that my hijab becomes a chador. I was 16 years old.

I am not allowed to listen to music anymore. Nor to smile. One day Noury sees me smile at a friend who is with some boys at the school exit. It's bad luck, usually it's the driver who comes to get me. The niqab is called "the windshield". Later, when I go to college, I will leave the house with it on, but I will take it off right away and put it back on before I get home. Of course, I still go to the mosque. I witness a fight. The imam stops preaching. Many men arrive. Noury goes to his car, comes back with sticks that he distributes to his friends and they beat a man who is lying on the ground. The blows make a strange soft noise. The man falls back, he does not shout. Noury, on the other hand, screams. He asks everyone to move aside, gets into his car, starts it up, and drives over the man's body. I think he is dead. He's my first dead person. On the way home, Noury tells me:

---

17. On the rise of the FIS and the black decade, Jean-Pierre Peyroulou wrote *History of Algeria since 1988* at La Découverte, 2020. The comment is complete and clear.
18. Many local elections were won by the Islamists before the 1990 legislative and presidential victories in 1991.

7. The raped child

"Did you see? This is what will happen to you if you are not a good Muslim."

I think it was 1992. Another time, Noury disappears for three days, I later understand that he was arrested by the police. When he returns, my grandmother says, "I hope they sat you on a bottle." I don't understand. Years later, I read in Horria Saïhi's beautiful testimony that this torture, inherited from the colonial war (Djamila Boupacha[19], for example, was a victim), was frequently used by the army against Islamists in the 1990s. On his way home, he has marks of beatings, but is even more angry than before.

At home, arguments are frequent. Noury is FIS, Moufid is FLN, Kadd, the antepenultimate of the family, is even a fervent communist! Lunches and dinners, in particular, are fights worthy of Arcady's films, without the good humor, but with more fear, because everyone is more or less afraid of Noury. This is how Moufid buys himself a small table to have dinner in his corner. Noury's other brothers are also engineers in gas, electricity and agronomy. Often the arguments get out of hand and my uncles fight physically, with their fists. I am afraid. The army is in the street all the time. This interweaving of fanaticism and a thousand other behaviors, rules of life or political ideologies, even within the village, the neighborhood or the community, is the rule in Algeria. Terrorism does not belong to this region or that population, it spreads by metastasis within the Algerian social stock, the family. From then on, a demarcation line is impossible to establish and fighting it becomes a challenge. Obviously, the Western

---

19. Djamila Boupacha, born in 1938. FLN activist, arrested, raped and tortured for weeks in 1960 by the French army, defended by Gisèle Halimi, sentenced to death and then amnestied at the last minute in 1962 when the Evian agreements were signed. Simone de Beauvoir published a text of support in the newspaper *Le Monde* entitled "Pour Djamila Boupacha" (For Djamila Boupacha) and then chaired her liberation committee. Her trial is considered the first major media trial of the post-war period.

world has not understood this, which has been determined to distinguish without nuance between the good and the bad. This is also the case in the Middle East, and of course the Western world still does not understand it.

One day, I was 16, I think, Noury took me to visit my in-laws. They tell me that I should be proud to marry a great warrior, a fighter for Allah. I don't want to. I say:

"I am against war and death."

The interview takes place in the garden of my promised. He has a little smile that I don't like, I feel like an object, an animal...

His mother, Genny, is French, he is Franco-Algerian. She says to me:

"You know, we're rich.

- I don't care, we're rich too," I said stupidly.

She takes me to the back of the estate to show me where we will live. It's a beautiful house.

As soon as we get home, I run to my grandmother. Noury told me that she agreed but I doubt it. Noury had just told me that we had to visit a friend. When we returned, Yemma asked:

"You were at the mosque?

- No, at a friend of Noury's with whom I have to get married but I don't want to," I said.

Noury tells him that I am promised anyway. And he mentions the big party at our house in 1986! I thought it was for my birthday. All this time I was promised to this man! My grandmother told me several times that I would never be forced into a marriage, like they used to do to girls. But even though I didn't know I was promised, I know about the practice and I suspect that Noury is in favor of it. And as he becomes more and more the boss at home... I repeat to my grandmother that I don't want to get married. Yemma manages to obtain a compromise: I will marry this man when I have finished my studies. In the family, the girls also study, even if this displeases Noury and his friends. I understood then that I had to study for a long time. I understand now why this anniversary was so great. After 1988 and Noury's total radicalization, my birthdays became completely "*haram*". I stay alone with my grandmother. I tell her that she has betrayed me, that I will be married anyway... She insists: the only way to postpone marriage is to go to university, that will at least give me a break.

"You have two choices," she summarizes in a tone that I find cynical: "You either marry him or you study."

I hope that Noury will agree to wait. Yemma is sinking into cynicism:

"Look on the bright side, if you marry a warrior, you could be a widow soon....

She leaves the sentence hanging.

- And I would be released? I said.

- Better," she smiled. You, the orphan, would inherit!"

On this subject, several times, Yemma told Noury that it was also necessary to ensure my future within the family."Orphan girl" is my nickname in the family, but Yemma doesn't use it often. I know that she arranged something at a notary's office for me, but Noury says that it doesn't matter, he decides everything. So Yemma tells me that I have to have a safe job to get by in life...

I'm determined to study, although I'm not sure what "getting out of trouble" would be in my situation.

Especially since life gets complicated: I'm in love!

8.
Life with death

"As paradoxical as it may seem, the decision to end one's life is a requirement of life to escape an undignified existence, behind bars, in a concentration camp."
Simon Critchley, *Suicide Letters*, Max Milo, 2015.

My phone vibrates. It's Eileen, Alia's mom. I contacted her several months ago on Instagram because her daughter's story is close to mine. Alia was abducted to Algeria by her father in 2016.

The story started out ordinary. Eileen is in love, she gets pregnant, but the father-to-be leaves her. He is a duplicitous man who has hidden from her that he is already married. Alia is born a few weeks later with a spinal cord malformation that requires care, money, frequent travel... Alone, Eileen faces with courage for months. Once the situation was stabilized, she decided to ask her ex-partner for custody rights so that she could look for a job. Eileen is a trained accountant. She likes her job. But this regularization frightens her ex, who fears having to pay alimony: "He completely lost his footing, he started to harass me, to blackmail me, to come and steal things from my house in my absence... " Eileen calls a lawyer. She filed a complaint. The situation became even more tense when the man was guilty, repeatedly, of not representing a child. After a "kidnapping" of more than one week which ends in a mediation of lawyers and a return of Alia to her mother, an opposition to the exit of the territory is arranged. Dying of fear, fearing that her father would kidnap Alia "for good", Eileen fled to Annecy, to her mother's home. However, she took care to leave an address for the father and an invitation to come and visit Alia. "Especially not to put me in my wrong", she thinks. The ex accepts a visit. It must be during the day, in a café, he will be able to spend time with his daughter but Eileen will be present. At the appointment, the drama is tied up on the carpark. The man snatches Alia from her mother, throws her in his car and escapes. Shocked, Eileen went back to the police station, reported the facts and specified that she was obviously afraid that her ex would take Alia away: "Don't rush," the police officer said, "we're not going to panic for nothing, he's her father, he has rights, he'll probably bring her back...". He was refused a new ban on leaving the country. A few hours later, Eileen received a text message: "I took Alia to Algeria. She went to the gendarmerie; this time her complaint was registered but nobody knew where to look for Alia. Since then, Eileen lives a hell. "It's all the more sad that we will learn later that he left only four days after sending me that text message, so if I had not been refused the second opposition of exit, we can think that Alia would not have been kidnapped." In 2019, her ex-partner is finally apprehended while trying to return to France. Eileen learns on this occasion that he has already returned several times, in defiance of the complaint filed. Tried and incarcerated, he simply declared to the investigators - who were satisfied - that "[the] mother was keeping her daughter in a place he did not know. Eileen went several times to Algeria, she could never obtain the recognition of the French court decision. She met a brother of her ex-partner "who refused to tell me where Alia was, and who made me understand that I was unworthy of having abandoned my daughter, but I suspected that my ex had told stories to his family, I said that I had been looking for her for more than four years, but for them I am not trustworthy, I am a woman and French, it is lost in advance. In France, the situation is blocked, in Algeria too. Currently in prison, Eileen's ex is patiently waiting for his release soon to return to Algeria. "Besides, he will have an OQTF (French Immigration and Temporary Stay Order)[20] , since he is not French, and I am very afraid that we will lose his trace for good, and therefore the trace of Alia.

Disregard for listening to women, underestimation of violence, administrative waste, incompetence, ignorance of risks, cumbersome procedures, interminable delays... Alia's case is exemplary[21] because it clearly leaves the impression that everything could have been easily avoided. And so I get angry, because she says that in 2022 the system does not work any better than it did in 1985, when I was abducted.

Annaba, summer 1990

My lover's name is Khalid. He is our next-door neighbor in another nice neighborhood where the family has an apartment. We went to school together, and often, in the evening, we played on the landing with Raf; well, when I could go out... Haya let us do that, but if Noury was there I had to go home. No way to be with boys, even as children. Today he has built a house by the sea. He is a banker and I still love him. His sister, Khalida, is from Paris, I see her from time to time.

20.Obligation to leave the French territory.
21.Alia's mother keeps a blog where she explains in detail the procedures launched, her attempts to find her daughter, but also the inefficiency of the research, the lack of support or perspectives... www.affairealiabouklachiwordpress.com

Khalid often comes to our house; he talks to me nicely. He is shy. It is inexplicable or almost but I believe that we had a love at first sight at 11 years old without knowing anything about love. It must happen from time to time, right? I immediately understand its interest. Without doubt, I, who have never received any, am better placed than anyone else to recognize and welcome the tenderness that his gaze sends me. When I sit on the sofa, he often takes a seat at the other end, at least one meter separates us, but no one, so it seems to me that this small unpopulated space connects us. Very quickly, there are small kisses. And then, when I was 15, one evening, it became more serious. I have a precise memory of it. It happens like this: it is the end of the afternoon, we are at Haya's house. I knew that Khalid was going to sleep there. This often happens after soccer games or when they have to study together. We are on the sofa, one meter away. Raf says he has to go buy a new ball before the store closes. I know he doesn't suspect anything. We are very attentive because we know that he would denounce us. Raf is a soccer fan, he follows the games, especially those of FC Annaba. Khalid plays music. Normally I am not allowed to, but when we are between us we don't care. He asks me if I want to dance with him. I say yes. We go towards each other, and it is the first time in my life that I am so close to a man who does not want to hurt me. I am veiled. I'm entranced by the music, or maybe it's Khalid. It's both. Peter Gabriel sings "Don't give up". Even today, not a day goes by without me listening to it. What I feel in contact with my childhood friend - what a strange word to use to talk about my childhood!- is a mixture of gentleness and confidence that I will never forget. And when he pushes back my veil to kiss me, it's as if I've lived my tiny life just waiting for that moment of eternity. We feel like we are doing something irreparable, and we are awkward like in an Emmanuel Mouret movie, but this moment of fullness intoxicates me, even though I have never drunk alcohol. I hold his hand. He looks at me. It is the first time he has seen me without a veil since I was 12. I cry with joy, this has never happened to me before. We don't go any further but we see each other more and more often. And, one day, Yemma pierces us. I don't dare to lie, I confide *that Khalid is nice and that I feel good when he is around.* I think she will get angry, maybe even talk to Noury. I don't mind being beaten again, but I will be deprived of Khalid.But no, Yemma is talking to us. I have the impression that she is happy, a little, to share something with us that Noury doesn't know: "You can go from here to there," she says, putting her hand flat under her chin, "but underneath it is forbidden, for *al-charaf.*" Honor is her domain, in Yemma, the honor of the family, which beats women, ignores crimes and locks up cuckolds. In plain English, this means that we can kiss each other but not touch each other lower than the chin. She doesn't say it explicitly, the Koran, *al-sharaf* and a thousand other laws forbid it - and honor too, no doubt - but we understand, despite our embarrassment. We didn't intend to, well I don't think so... Above all," Yemma insists, "let Noury never find out." The next day, Yemma points to one of the drivers and tells me that she has spoken to him, he will protect us, take us for a walk, stay in the next room when Khalid comes, "provided that you respect the rules." I lower my head:

"Thank you."

Over the years, this love has only grown stronger. This is why I feel doubly betrayed by Yemma's lukewarm reaction when she learns, or pretends to learn, that Noury has promised me to a fighter from Afghanistan. Yemma knows nothing of my love. I remind her all the same:

"You know I love Khalid."

She says that it is an additional problem and that this boy, who will obviously know soon that I am promised, should not dare to come to ask for my hand, too, because that would make a scandal with Noury who would surely become violent. But I don't care about Noury's violence! Of course, I told Khalid about it as soon as I could isolate myself for a while with him at school. He decided to talk to his father about it. A few days later, they would both come and ask for my hand in marriage.

Khalid's father was an important executive of a large gas company. His family is not as powerful as "mine", but much more free. They drink aperitifs, for example, without hiding. At home, they know it and they are reproached for it. When Khalid's father calls Noury, my guardian agrees to receive them, but he knows that he will refuse the request. And so do I.

They come one evening around 6 pm. We settle down in the living room. It is Khalid who speaks, it is not done. He says that he loves me and wants to marry me. The day before, we met, he is sure that he can convince Noury, that there is no objective reason to refuse, that maybe Noury will put conditions but he will be able to comply... This is what happens. Noury tells him that he is a miscreant, his family is a miscreant, and that to convince him to "start thinking" he should join the FIS and go to the mosque every day. This is obviously impossible. Khalid says he is a believer in his own way. Noury adds that I have been promised since 1986.

In this case," intervenes Khalid's father, "why did you let us do it? It doesn't make sense.

- Just being polite," Noury replies.

The situation becomes inextricable and dangerous. And the tone rises very quickly. Questioned about religion and asked again to join the Islamist party, Khalid answers that he will never be "on the side of the cutthroats". End of the discussion. Noury sends them back home and forbids Khalid to approach me. After their departure, Noury comes to see me in my room where I took refuge. He knows nothing about my relationship with Khalid. Yemma didn't tell him about it, I'm sure, otherwise I would have been beaten up long ago. But he is suspicious, he wants to know more. While I am crying, he explains to me that he let him come to convert him, as it is his duty as a Muslim.

I discover that my blondness and my cursed sixteen spring are well coveted. The next day, informed undoubtedly by the Arab telephone, my cousin Raf and his father ring the doorbell without having warned. Noury obviously receives his brother-in-law, who explains to him that he asks me for his son, that Raf wants me, and that he must benefit from a right of priority because he is the elder of the cousins. Tragic vaudeville. In any case, Noury says:

"I promised, I can't go back."

My cousin Raf's father is the CEO of the company that employs Khalid's father, and he proposes to fire him and even cut off his electricity if Khalid "hangs around our daughter again". He says "our daughter": I belong to everyone but myself. At least, this time, I am relieved that he refused: every time I sleep at Haya's, Raf comes to stick me during the night, a bit like he does, even if it is less... I don't add that, but I say anyway that "once I kicked him in the crotch to make him stop". Noury looks at me hard and says:

"He did that because you surely provoked him", and he beats me. Yemma, alerted by my cries, arrives in the kitchen, I take refuge behind her. She protects me, and Noury stops, it happens sometimes. A little later, I explain the case in detail to Yemma, she reproaches me for having spoken to Noury:

"But finally, it was you who told me that Khalid should not caress me, but Raf, yes?"

In general, my confidence in my grandmother is waning greatly. I am growing up. Maybe I don't need the denial anymore, I also see her cowardice...

The following week, offended, my cousin Raf will provoke Khalid to fight. Khalid, who is not a fighter, will take blows. To calm down the game, we will decide to see each other less. At the time, it seemed to me a common decision.

And Yemma dies.

9.
Escape, temptation and attempts

"The lot of the superior woman is the absolute desert. She knows only the bitter fruit of originality, the hatred of others, she pays for her revolt against the social order with solitude [...]. Whoever is really worthy of freedom does not wait to be given it, he takes it."
Andrée Dore-Audibert and Annie Morzelle, *Révolutionnaires silencieuses au xxe siècle,* Éd. Kerdoré, 1991.

Azz, Noury's brother, lived in London. He has a fiancée there and it is said in the family that he returned to Algeria and left her pregnant. It is also said that the main reason for his return was a fight in a pub that got out of hand and during which he killed a man with a knife.

In Algeria, Azz mellowed for a while before making a comeback by marrying the biggest prostitute in the Tête Rouge district, the brothel district of Annaba. When Yemma told me half-heartedly about Azz's past - he never told me about it, and neither did Noury - I thought it was a beautiful irony, for someone who did not want to marry and had refused an English woman, to marry an Algerian whore. Azz broke the news around 1990, during a dinner party where the whole family was gathered. Moufid exclaimed:

"But you're crazy, we all fucked her!"

This made one more conflict at home, from which Azz was excluded after a kind of family council.

Azz will continue to see his mother once or twice a month, he comes to pick her up, he stays outside, she goes out, they go for a walk, she comes back, he leaves. Yemma herself refuses to see his wife, and even more so that she moves into the family home: "This whore will never live in my property. This whore nevertheless arrives on the day of Yemma's death in the family home. She smiles. It is the day of revenge for her, and as if to be well understood in the insult that she intends to address by her presence to the deceased herself, she puts on the traditional wedding dress, the garment of the cursed marriage, which Yemma refused to endorse. When I see her, at the threshold of the death chamber, I say to her, with tears in my eyes:

"You don't have the right to be here.

She looks at me:

- Now that she's dead, Azz is going to come back and he'll get his share and so it's my place too."

I am not interested in their inheritance stories, but the insult to my grandmother revolts me. I shout, I push her, I can't control my rage. Noury arrives, I know that his hatred against her will be stronger, or at least take precedence, over his habit of beating me at the slightest opportunity. So he makes me go into the kitchen with his wife, Noura.

But my rage has no limits. I also go after Noura:

"You have always despised her," I said.

It is true. Everyone knows that Noura, Noury's wife, despised Yemma, because Noury is the strongest in the family.

Yemma's illness did not come on suddenly, but little by little she became bedridden. Noura made her life difficult, forbidding the servants to approach her to wash her. Haya, Noury's sister, was not often there. I used to wash her when I got home from school, but sometimes I arrived late, so Yemma spent a lot of time dirty. Noura could even leave her thirsty all day. Several times I found her glass empty on her bedside table, her lips dry. She was asking for a drink.

"Why didn't you ask Noura?" Silence. I knew Noura was pretending not to hear.

"Why didn't you ask your many daughters-in-law?" Silence. She probably didn't want to disturb.

Once, I find her on the floor in the laundry room next to a basin with a pair of panties stained with menstrual blood. It can't be Yemma's, so it's Noura's. Her daughter-in-law is next to her, but she doesn't see me, she is leaning against the washing machine. She simply washes her stained underwear. I immediately understand that it is about humiliating her. Her look expresses all the arrogance and contempt she feels for her husband's mother, defeated by the years and the course of life. Her look changes as soon as I enter, which immediately makes me angry because I understand that she is aware of the harm she is imposing on Yemma. It is psychological torture, and it is voluntary. I know what she is doing and she knows that I know. I tell Yemma that we will call the doctor. My grandmother is a little delirious, she is afraid, at this time, that Noury will throw her out into the street. "It's your uncles who have the power and the money." In a fit of anger, I hit Noura, I put her head in the basin. And I take Yemma back to bed.

When Noury returned, Noura called her into the room where she had retreated. I understand what is going to happen, I am ready for it, but I will not give in. When Noury enters the living room where Yemma and I are sitting, I tell her:

"I know you're going to hit me, I don't care, Noura wanted to humiliate Yemma, she's leading you around by the nose and you should be defending your mother."

9. Escape, temptation and attempts

I try to continue with the story of the events and the episode of the soiled linen, but he beats me up in front of my grandmother, who shouts and hits the floor with her cane. When I manage to take refuge in my room, I am out of breath and resistance. But the anger is so strong that I break a window pane. I hurt myself.

This was the time when Noury lost all control of his violence. One day, when I had to iron his shirts before going to school, he reproached me for a tiny crease under a button. He jumps on me and beats me. I screamed. It was so violent that my aunt Naadi, who lived above me with my uncle Moufid, came down and interfered. It is rare.

Another time, four of my uncles, I don't remember which ones but there was Noury and Azz for sure, hit me at the same time while I was rolling on the floor. I don't even know why they beat me this time. But I remember that I was saved by my father who, on leave from the hospital, arrived at that time to pay us a visit. He pulled me away from them and took me with him. We spent a few hours together. We went for a walk on the beach, but he had to take me back.

There is no excuse for Noury's criminal behavior, of course, but I am aware that I have often provoked him. I am not insolent, I am naturally insubordinate. I find that a quality. Not Noury.

On the day of Yemma's funeral, there are at least two hundred people at the house. Noury is busy in an assembly that includes several of his friends. I approach him and ask him straight out:

"Why do you and your family keep me prisoner since you don't like me and I do everything wrong? Especially since you know I want to go back to France!"

The little group stares at me, probably wondering how I dare challenge Noury, and perhaps pondering a situation they don't know about that gives them an unknown intimate fact about their mentor. But, deep down, this is a question that has really been nagging at me for a long time. My attitude is always disturbing, they accuse me of disgracing them, of not being able to follow any rule (the last one they impose on me is not to eat fruit anymore, I don't know why, Noury decided that it was impure, except for dates, which, unfortunately, I only like in *makrout*[22] or *mesfouf*[23]). My intervention makes Noury very angry but he holds back, obviously. Doesn't he dare to hit me in front of so many people? Usually he is the kind of person who dares to do anything. Here, he is even conciliatory, and says:

"But you know you always had a choice, you can go live with my sister Haya, for example.

I have been waiting for this proposal to deliver the stab:

- But you know that my cousin Raf comes to stick and rub against me at night, just like you do.

It breaks down into:

- And by the way, daddy told you not to rub on me like that anymore, why don't you stop?

Noury is livid. It's madness, I'm signing my death warrant, but I insist:

- You refused to let me marry Raf, and that's fine, but you want to send me there?No, let me go back to France!

He can't stand it anymore. I see his hand rise but I feel it as a victory. He hits me on the cheek and then drops me. The punches and kicks rain down. He literally slaughters me in front of his friends. I don't have any illusions but I tell myself that maybe someone will try to stop him... Nothing. Between the volleys of blows, I perceive, with the comments of the guests, that everyone is against me:

"It's well done.

- Insolent.

22.Cake filled with dates and cinnamon.
23.Sweet Berber Couscous.

9. Escape, temptation and attempts

- French bitch.

Azz is there. I manage to get up and I say to him:

- Even you don't say anything, you could defend me, you who also have a humiliated but free wife."

Almost paralyzed by the bruises, it will take days before I can leave my room.

A few months later, I escaped again: in January 1993, I managed to hide in a train to Tunis. My plan was to go to Yemma's sister's house. I passed the first control, hidden in the toilet, but I was surprised by the second. I gave my Algerian identity card, the customs officer had a dirty look in his eyes, both salacious and dominating:

"You know you're not allowed to travel alone..."

I have the presence of mind to say that my tutor was with me but that he had to return to Annaba because he is sick. I go to my uncle's house... "It's okay," the official tells me as he turns away. Two hours later, I arrived hungry and thirsty in Tunis. The first thing I do, once I cross the border, is to remove my veil. I know that in Tunisia it is not compulsory, I even think that at the time it was forbidden. I feel a sense of freedom that I have never experienced before. I walk for a good hour before arriving at Belvedere, where my great-aunt and her family live. When I knock on the door, I am exhausted. My great-uncle opens the door, he understands right away. He welcomes me. I was exhausted.

We have dinner and I go to sleep with my cousins. I wake up in the middle of the night screaming, "Don't cut our throats! Don't cut our throats!" with my hands on my throat. One of my cousins wakes up with a start. I stammer apologies, still in shock from a nightmare whose details I will never forget - the terrorists' knives, their cynical smiles, my offered throat... - nor the fear it inspired in me. She retorts, half-serious, half-amused:

"No, no, don't worry, here we're not going to cut your throat."

This nightmare will take me back to Paris after the Bataclan attack.

The next morning, when I wake up, Noury is waiting for me in the kitchen.

He came alone, by car.

I make a move to retreat to my cousin's room. I feel like the world is crumbling under my feet. I am going to faint. My great-aunt holds me back and helps me sit up.

Noury is already shouting:

"Put your veil back on, you little bitch!

But my great-uncle intervenes:

- No. Don't veil yourself, it's forbidden here.

And to Noury, he asks to be quiet:

- Noury, we respect your authority, but this little girl is lost, she comes to me for help. She is of my blood, but even if she were not, I would welcome her. I ask you to let her stay with us for a while.

- I am his legal guardian," says Noury.

- Yes," my great-uncle replied, "but here you are also considered a terrorist and I ask you to think carefully about the situation. My great-uncle is a smart man, he manages to threaten Noury without making him lose face. Noury agrees that I should spend a little "vacation" in Tunisia. He left with a last look of murder.

I will spend a month of rest and peace with them. I will ask them to help me to return to France, my great-uncle and great-aunt will refuse without even taking the necessary steps:

"Sorry, we can't do that, because of the family."

They fear Noury, like everyone else.

In Tunis, I discovered a new freedom, but then, if I couldn't go back to Paris, maybe I could stay here to study sociology? A new, more embarrassed refusal from the family:

"You have a home, you have to make concessions with them... Besides, time is running out, we're going to have to take you back soon."

Later, I would learn that Noury was threatening his uncle with a lawsuit in Algeria and "no one had any interest in that". Obviously, compassion and hospitality have their limits. Noury's power, however, does not.

When I arrived in Annaba, I felt like I was back in hell. I was beaten from the day I arrived, then almost every day, for any reason. Fortunately, Khalid is there and I can see him from time to time. Life is reorganizing itself despite everything. The driver that Yemma trusted becomes my driver. I often go to Khalid's house under the pretext that I am going to see Khalida, his sister. When another driver or Noury takes me there, they check that Khalid is not in the house, especially if I have to stay overnight, which happens from time to time. At the beginning, Haya comes to check and then her checks become less frequent.

And chance gets involved.

One day, while leaving Khalid's house, I see Mouloud's father in the street. I recognize him at once, it is at his place that Mouloud left my sisters. We smile at each other, but we can't talk because a driver is with me. I enter a clothes store and tell the driver to wait for me, I hope that Pépé (I also call him Pépé, like Annie's father, my grandfather from France) will follow me. It is indeed the case. We talk. He asks me how I am, he seems sincerely happy to see me. I say that I'm not doing well, obviously. He tells me that my mother has been in Algiers for a few months now and that she has taken my sisters who were living with him. I tell him about my Tunisian escapade. I talk about Noury's violence. I say that I have been looking for years for a way to end it, either I escape or I die. I see that my story touches him, he offers to help me get my French papers back:

"I know where they are, I can bring them to you, Mouloud keeps them, but I can take them."

Hope is reborn. We agree on a stratagem to see each other again, in order to multiply our chances, because I don't go out much: Pepe will come to several successive appointments, in several stores, spread over several days. I will find a way to come ! To make it more credible, I put Khalid and his sister in the confidence. Khalida places several orders in these stores for the following week. We can go out. The day of the first appointment, I see Pepe in the street but I am accompanied by a hostile driver. No way. The second appointment is the right one. I ask the complicit driver to wait for me at the door. We enter the store. Pepe hands me an envelope with the papers and says:

"If you want, I can set up a meeting with your mother."

10.
The meeting

"Let's keep hope, the worst is yet to come!"
Bernard Bretonnière, *On n'a jamais fini de ranger la vaisselle*,
Éd. Pneumatiques, 2020.

Yesterday, I went to do some archival research at the Algerian cultural center. For 42 euros of photocopying and binding, I gathered a two hundred page file of press articles that deal with the subject of parental kidnappings between France and Algeria, particularly in the eighties and nineties. And last night I read the file. There are several constants. In the Algerian press, one begins almost systematically by deploring the "loss of values" of modern societies, which leads to situations of rupture, "sad divorces[24] " but still "sometimes neces-sary[25] ". In short, a value judgment on the moral decay of men, and especially of women of course, modern, decay that is condemned in infantilizing terms through maxims of common school: "The love of parents is a noble sentiment", "A child loves his father as much as

---

24.Ghania Mouffok, " Couples mixtes, au nom du fils ", *Algérie-Actualité*, n° 1032 25-31 July 1985.
25."An issue, the custody of the child", *El Moujahid,* 04-12-1985.

his mother"[26]... Then comes regularly the strongest argument: the Algerians, the society, the Algerian law, have things to say on the subject, and their position has naturally the same value as that of their French or European counterparts. We denounce the eurocentric vision of the problem, "whose deep foundations refer to the belief - oh so tenacious - of the superiority of the Judeo-Christian civilization[27] ". In fact, the paradigm most frequently considered by French society is that of a mother from whom an Arab father kidnaps her children to take refuge in Algeria and forbid the mother the slightest access to her offspring. This is, more or less, my case. But the problem has multiple aspects. There are many cases of fathers being cheated, of visiting rights being granted to mothers followed by "non-representation" of children, which legally constitutes a second abduction, and even of children being abducted in Algeria and brought back to France, in clear violation of Algerian law[28].

There is an Algerian right and it has something to say. In particular, he deplores the fact that the deterioration of bilateral relations and, very clearly, the rise of xenophobic ideas, the return to the forefront of subjects that were thought to have been evacuated forever, such as "the benefits of colonialism", or the increasingly generous place given to the theses of the racist extreme right in France, have prevented progress towards a lasting resolution. For Anaïs, this is even an essential aspect of the problem. As Algeria does not adhere to the Hague Convention, the resolution of parental abduction situations between our two countries inevitably goes through the consular channel and depends, *in fine,* on political or diplomatic hazards. The legal

---

26.*Ibid.*
27.Ghania Mouffok, " Couples mixtes, au nom du fils ", *Algérie-Actualité*, n° 1032 25-31 July 1985.
28.On legal kidnapping, see the next chapter.

framework for an abduction, when there is no Hague Convention or bipartite agreement[29]," explains my friend, "is Brussels II ter[30], but, in order to be applied, this regulation presupposes judicial cooperation, which may be lacking. The starting point is therefore the recognition by the country "of destination" of the abduction, of the French judicial decision and its opposability, "but the exéquatur[31] quickly finds itself dependent on the circumstances, the history, the relations between the two countries, especially when it is a question of Algeria, taking into account the colonial past. Too much affect and not enough law.

For example, Emmanuel Macron went to Algeria twice: the first time in 2017, to look for money that Bouteflika's clique gave him for his presidential campaign, and also to declare that colonization was "a crime against humanity". The second time in 2022, to look for gas that was not sold to him, and also to declare that colonization was "a love story". The ministers, the judges, the Algerian people, hear these speeches. They provoke or suffer the effects of it. Nothing will go in the right direction as long as France holds this neo-colonial paternalistic position towards Algeria. Nothing. In fact, the 1988 text, signed by Georgina Dufoix for the Socialist government of Laurent Fabius, but prepared by Pierre Mauroy since 1981, which is still the reference in this matter, relied on the renewed links with Algeria and a less hostile climate in France to propose significant progress. On

---

29. Indeed, the 1988 convention serves as a bipartite agreement, but its implementation still depends very much on the goodwill of the states. Judicial cooperation is not automatic.

30. The European Brussels II bis Regulation of March 2005, revised in 2019 to become II ter, establishes a framework for the "recognition and enforcement of judgments in matrimonial matters and in matters of parental responsibility, as well as in matters of international child abduction". It applies in the absence of a bipartite agreement or accession to the Hague Convention.

31. The exequatur is the procedure aiming at giving, in a State, enforceability to a judgment made abroad.

this subject, Annie Sugler, head of a mothers' association[32], noted in 1988 that the agreement was only possible because "high-level political leaders from both sides of the Mediterranean" had managed to talk to each other, as she had long been demanding. Under the terms of this historic agreement between France and Algeria, there would never again be a possibility of "abduction" by either parent of a child "born to a separated Franco-Algerian couple". The text decides that the competent jurisdiction will be that of the country where the child's domicile is located "at the time of the break-up", i.e. France when the children are abducted in France, and no longer of the marital domicile, which was a notion frequently interpreted by the courts of "destination countries" as "the new place where the father has decided to settle".

But, wedged between two paragraphs, the essential sentence of the text says that "court judgments will be accompanied by an automatic authorization to leave the territory", which means "that one will not be able to evoke the paternal opposition for the non-execution of the court decisions". The repatriating parents being most often the fathers, this provision takes all its sense in the Algerian case, because if the Algerian law recognizes well that "the right of custody can be entrusted to the mother", it accompanies this eventuality of a devious provision: "... but the maintenance, the schooling and the education of the child must be done in the religion of the father". It is on this sentence that the fathers' lawyers relied to justify the refusal to "return" the children. This provision, in the form of a lawsuit of intent, was obviously impossible to guarantee in advance. The 1988 convention is therefore an agreement to protect children, but there is a long way to go... ".In French law, it is rarely the source that is missing. The

---

32.Collective for the defense of abducted children.

texts are often there, they are often good, even if they can always be improved, but the problem is in the application". In short, the agreement does not guarantee judicial cooperation, yet this is really where we need to make progress: "We need real mutual legal assistance that is imposed on politics." But for Anaïs, and of course for ThéraVie ARP-APA anti-RPicide, the key to the problem lies upstream: better centralization and circulation of information, better detection and follow-up of identified cases, extended powers of intervention... I will read in the exhibits placed in the file of the divorce judgment of my genitrix and Mouloud a hallucinating letter from Mouloud to the judge in which he announces by antiphrases - in the mode "I don't want to do it but I could" - my kidnapping! I can't help but think that a social worker might have been moved by this... " It's very true, confirms Anja.It is very right, confirms Anaïs, but it would be necessary to give them the means, and they are overwhelmed, I had one in my office yesterday who was dealing with twenty children's files, it is unmanageable!

At the European level, there is also a hotline number, 116 000, which allows to report any abduction or even any threat of abduction. The first step to take afterwards is to file a substantiated complaint, which must contain proof of the parental authority of the parent filing the complaint. But here again," explains Anaïs, "the planets have to align because even if we notice that a child is not being represented, we have to report it quickly, specifying that the offending parent could take the child out of France, that the family court judge (JAF) acts quickly and that we pass on the information to the border police... the injunction refusing to take the child out of the country is only valid for fifteen days.

Generally speaking, countries that harbor abducted children systematically argue first about the need to take legal action at home (and cry racism or neo-colonialism if the abducted parent refuses). This process is a trap because it prevents any future recourse in the event of an unfavorable judgment against the despoiled parent. The recent case of Sylvain and Arslan Roy, his son[33], is exemplary in this regard. This father, whose son was kidnapped in France in 2017 by his Kazakh mother (thanks to a false passport, a false baptismal certificate and, again, the scandalous laxity of the French border police[34]), has been offered several times a trial in Astana by the authorities of the mother's country. He has always refused. For him, "it is a trap, the trial is lost in advance", because because of the corruption and the natural tendency of the judges to give in to the arguments of the Kazakh mother "such a trial risks to close definitively the door to any action". Indeed, if the court establishes the mother's right, no French diplomatic or judicial action will be admissible anymore. End of the tragedy.

The 1988 text also provides for the creation of a joint commission to study disputes and cases in dispute, and then to give its opinion to the courts, which will decide.

My sisters and I are a "contentious". On my own, I represent a double dispute since I am also a "natural" child in the eyes of Algerian law and the French convention. I am "illegitimate" in addition to being repatriated. It is frequent that Algerian judges return illegitimate children to their mothers. Natural, they are immoral, born of

---

33. Sources Origines.media Instagram account and *Nice-Matin* article of 26-04-2022.
34. It is not a question here of criticizing, in the wake of the French right and extreme right, an alleged "absence of border controls" which would be responsible for the arrival of millions of migrant invaders on our Gallic soil, but rather of reversing this criticism: we systematically control foreigners who enter France "on the face", but a Kazakh (or Algerian or Congolese...) citizen who leaves the territory with crude false documents, that disturbs the customs officers much less. I can't help but see a similarity with the way I was abducted. In my case, too, the customs officer did not ask many questions. First of all, we were Arabs returning to Algeria.

an anti-religious alliance, they are the mark of sin, and Algeria does not want them. My paradoxical misfortune is that I was not returned, despite my illegitimate status, probably because, a lawyer told me much later, I had been kidnapped at the same time as my sisters and Algerian law had legally "confused" my case with theirs... Everything was already so complex, they were not going to take a personal interest in each child... [35]

Since I haven't slept, I prefer to cancel my psych session this morning. I never do, but this will be too hard. The sessions are busy and demanding. Technically, I have PTSD (post-traumatic stress disorder). I'm in CBT (cognitive behavioral therapy). And I also have dissociative amnesia, which we try to treat with cognitive remediation. When you are exposed to a lot of trauma, your brain creates "alters", like different characters in the same body. This is called a "dissociative identity disorder". That's why I have amnesia, because if an alter takes over, we say "it's at the front", it perceives and exposes memories, but when another one takes its place, it perceives and exposes its own memories while hiding the previous ones. In other words, I have forgotten a lot of serious things that happened to me and I am trying to remember them to rebuild myself. But it's complicated because a lot of serious things have happened to me! From time to time, a drama comes to mind that would be enough to fill a lifetime of psychoanalysis! For example, I had forgotten to talk to my co-author about the meeting of 1988, although it is a turning point in my history! I can feel that it annoyed him but I don't do it on purpose, I am dissociated! My memories are partial, truncated, like those of the man on the Orly pier in Chris Marker's film. It's at the end that

---

35. The distinction between legitimate and illegitimate children appears as it is in the report by Senator Guy Cabanel. See also the following chapter.

we understand. I forgot to talk about this encounter and yet I have a physical, material, sensory memory of it. It is in me.

Well, I'm talking about it now.

It started with a phone call.

Annaba, May or June 1988

It's my uncle Moufid who picks up. I am next to him, in the living room. I don't understand the conversation, but his discomfited and worried look when he hangs up seriously concerns me. Something serious has happened. As I know I won't be answered, I don't ask any questions, but I observe, bewildered, the panic that takes hold of everyone. As we were to spend the day at home, at least until the cool of the evening, I catch some words from Noury to Yemma:

"We have to leave, we're going to the desert, fast!"

The time to load the car with some badly made bags, the engine is already running. Noury is driving, Azz is in front, I am in the back, next to Moufid. Yemma stayed at home. In bits and pieces, I catch the words *police, faster, desert...* But no sooner have we turned the corner than a police car, all sirens blaring, corners us against the sidewalk. I am very afraid. The Bs, Mouloud's family, are also very powerful. Noury knows all the religious leaders, Yemma speaks with the president, he even came to our house. If we are arrested, it means that something very serious is going on.

Yemma runs over. She keeps me out of the discussion between Noury and the police. But a few minutes later, my tutor comes to us and explains to her mother that "we have to do it this time". I am very careful never to speak Arabic and I never intervene in their exchanges because the fact that I understand it a little gives me a useful advantage.

An hour later, the time to give some instructions to the house and to prepare a viaticum, Noury, Yemma and I embark in the police car. That evening, we met in a big hotel in the center of the capital. Everyone is worried. We sleep in the same room. Noury snores, but I sleep well.

The next morning, just after breakfast, we go to a big hall and the first thing I see in the middle of the crowd is my sisters... I burst into tears as I run towards her. Noury tries to hold me back but I turn around and violently twist his arm with all my strength. His hand rises, but he does not dare... I run, my sisters fall into my arms and it takes the gentleness and patience of Yemma, perhaps moved too, to separate us. Then I raise my eyes towards the spectacle which had escaped me, obsessed as I was by Fleur and Rose that I find after more than three years.

Dozens of people, hundreds perhaps, come and go, greet each other, exchange, and even for some, seem to find each other as I found my sisters. There are children everywhere, nearly two hundred, I will learn a little later. I understand that they are families and I obviously make the connection with my personal situation, to the point of caricature: these crying women are mothers, these men on guard are fathers or guardians, these haggard children awaken in me a penetrating feeling of joy and sadness all at once. I recognize myself in them. So I am not alone. I hope that not all of them have experienced what I have. In the middle of this hubbub, some people move with more ease than others, they are surely leaders, men most often, they have ties and suits. Some women too, European, seem important. There are also some lawyers in robes, and dozens of men and women with microphones, cameras, notebooks, running around.

I didn't see them at first glance, but Annie and Mouloud are there, obviously. They accompany my sisters. I haven't seen them since the beginning of the school year in 1985, when Annie came to explain to me that my kidnapping was my fault, and Mouloud showed up drunk at the wheel of his Mercedes, screaming that he wanted to marry me. Mouloud embraced me. Not Annie. Then they go to Noury. I have the impression that they talk to each other like accomplices.

Much later, I would recognize, in a newspaper article, a photo of Mouloud in discussion with a journalist. The caption explains that he is defending the fathers' point of view: "The children must stay in Algeria." Even today, many lawyers, starting with Linda Weil-Curiel, who handled the Mothers of Algiers[36], believe that each situation of a repatriated child must be studied individually. The principle that links them all is uprooting. So, according to them, repatriating, ten or fifteen years after his abduction, an adolescent who has sometimes unlearned his native language and seems to have forgotten his mother, no longer makes sense. It is a double uprooting, which perhaps the children themselves no longer want. For the mothers, it is an additional pain.

Mouloud has never shown me the same violence as Annie or Noury. But as I read this, I think I could strangle him: he and Annie are in France, drinking, doing drugs and spending my father's money, while my sisters and I are languishing in Algeria with our respective grandmothers. Of course, my sisters will never be physically abused. But we are all there against our will. Of these cursed years, which also

---

36. On November 9, 1983, while President Chadli Bendjedid was on an official visit to France, a delegation of French women went to the Algerian embassy in Paris. They belonged to the National Association for the Defense of Abducted Children (ANDEE) and intended to alert public opinion to the parental abduction of which they and their children were victims. See also Chapter 4.

correspond to the period of her adultery with Beny, Annie will say one day that they were the most beautiful of her life...

There is also a photo of me, published by a magazine, where I am shown with my sister Fleur, sitting against a wall. You can't see it, but Noury is standing, watching us. Yemma is next to me. It is taken just before we enter the small office. But why are we in this huge room? Why are my sisters here? I questioned Mouloud but his answer rather worried me:

"You'll see, shut up."

Soon enough, I understand, as I see children and parents enter in turn a small office at the back of the room, guarded by lawyers, that each family must be interviewed. To say what? Am I going to be asked something?

My grandmother leans over to me and speaks in my ear. Suddenly my name echoes in the immense space. Our turn has come. I have never experienced anything so impressive. There is a desk behind which two people are sitting, whom I call ministers, one is French, the other Algerian, it seems. Other people are standing behind them. I sit in front of the desk, facing them. My sisters sit on either side of me. Behind me, a hand on each of my shoulders, Mouloud and Noury. My mother between them. I think back to Yemma's words.

The French minister speaks first. I have no recollection of what he says. But I will never forget the question that ends his speech. He turns to me, looks me in the eye and says:

"Do you want to stay here or go back to France?"

11.
The choice? What choice?

"Happiness is always for the next shot!"
Bernard Bretonnière, *On n'a jamais fini de ranger la vaisselle*,
Éd. Pneumatiques, 2020.

"Hello, Madam, my story is very similar to yours. I am currently in Ivory Coast[37] and I want to return to France. I am French but my story is very complicated. My father kidnapped me and my sister. I received the first message from Pearl in June 2021. We communicate through social networks. I am almost her only contact with "the outside world". For more than ten years, she has been held captive by her father. For her too, things were first presented in a legal light. African father, French mother. Divorce. Her father returns to Africa, Pearl and her sister stay in France with their mother, according to the divorce decree. When the mother falls ill, the father returns to France and takes charge of Pearl's and her sister's education at the mother's home. A year later, the mother died and, without telling anyone, the father took the girls to Africa. "He told us we were going away for the vacations." Obviously, he has no intention of bringing them back.

37.Names and places are fictitious to protect children.

The case is complex because the father has parental authority, even if the divorce decree has fixed the girls' residence in France. Today, as an adult, Pearl is still stuck in Ivory Coast. Her father confiscated her papers. Last month, I sent her the detailed process to retrieve her birth certificate via the Internet, but her web access is too limited. The girls are deprived of going out, making phone calls, contacting strangers, communicating with their mother or France. Despite the difficulties, Pearl managed to go to the French consulate but they refused to take any steps to certify Pearl's and her sister's French nationality without... a document proving their French nationality. Kafkaesque situation. In Créteil, I contacted her aunt who succeeded, thanks to a kind lady at the registry office, to apply for a birth certificate in triplicate, one of which must imperatively arrive at the embassy in Abidjan. Pearl's sister is 11 years old, I already know that it will be very very difficult for her, but I haven't told her yet.

Faced with a wall of inaction, some families resort to legal kidnapping. This is a double-edged sword. I always want to defend this argument of justice and morality, but the first thing to say on the subject is that it is very perilous, for the child first, for the parents, and for the hope that one day we will manage to give a real status to the kidnapped children and a legal framework to settle the great majority of the cases Legal kidnapping takes several forms. First, there is the case of a child with visiting rights whose mother does not return. The most famous case is that of Salim, which nearly scuttled the 1988 Convention[38]. Then there is the incredible and very dangerous possibility of the

---

38. Case of Salim: arrived in France at Christmas 1987 to spend the holidays with his mother, within the framework of a right of visit, obtained following a hunger strike of several mothers, and for which the Algerian government had to operate pressure by body on the father, the child was not presented to the return. "It's my decision," said Salim. But the matter seriously undermined the ongoing negotiations. The father turned, victoriously, against the Algerian state.

child being located in Algeria - or in any other country where he or she is kept repatriated - and then being abducted and repatriated to France. Beyond the trauma for the child[39], frequent and never really considered by the parent who is willing to use this stratagem, the consequences, in case of failure, are disastrous: the child's removal, loss of contact, trial, prison... It is a trick that is played only once, and that fails most of the time. The Quai d'Orsay officially disapproves of this method of action, but the hypocrisy lies in the fact that French law actually recognizes it, since it is technically a child who escapes from his kidnappers! A third ministry also has something to say. In January 1988, the Ministry of Women's Rights, through the voice of Yvette Roudy[40], condemned the attitude of Salim's mother and appealed to the "sense of responsibility of mothers" who receive their abducted children with visiting rights. We thus find ourselves in the ubiquitous situation where two ministries of the French government condemn an act committed on foreign territory, while another one legally ratifies it! In 1984, *Le Nouvel Observateur*[41] recalls the case of Marie-Noëlle and her father, who arrived in Algeria a first time in 1981, then again in 1984, in order to "kidnap" Marie-Noëlle's son from his "father-ravisor". The adventure ends in prison and causes a diplomatic incident. And the distress of the families feeds a "business". A Swiss association, the Movement Against Child Abduction, even claims to

---

39.The only study produced on the traumatic effects on abducted children was published in 2014 by Marilyn Freeman of the NGO International Center for Family Law, Policy and Practice.

40.Born in 1929, Minister of Women's Rights from 1981 (ministry created by François Mitterrand) to 1985. The 1982 law on the reimbursement of abortion and the 1983 law on gender equality bear her name. Signer, in April 1971 in *Le Nouvel Observateur*, of the petition written by Simone de Beauvoir, of the 343 women declaring to have had an abortion, petition known as "Manifesto of the 343 sluts".

41.Mariella Righini, " Paris-Alger, des enfants sans mères ", *Le Nouvel Observateur*, 13-07-84.

have repatriated some fifty children abducted in the 1980s. Similarly, the French detective Serge Muller[42] developed "military techniques" to bring back children, before being caught by the French justice system for "possession of administrative documents", a pretext which caused the end of his "career" but which reinforced his convictions: "The children write to me, for them I am the 'uncle'", or: "Look at this one: "I often think of you". Other associations flourish on the Internet, most of them scandalously exploiting the pain of families.

And then there is an aspect of the problem that is neglected because it is not politically correct. At the time of the signing of the bilateral convention, and even in the nineties and two thousand, it was the fathers who kidnapped the children. Today, the multiplication of mixed marriages and the increase in the phenomenon of religious traditionalization of women have resulted in a significant increase in abductions by mothers. The phenomenon is still marginal in Algeria, but already much more marked in the Middle East and Egypt. We are not ready, neither on one side of the Mediterranean nor on the other.

A few weeks ago, I found a report by Senator Guy Cabanel[43]. He is a pied-noir and the subject interests him. He worked with Georgina Dufoix on the draft convention. After noting that France had worked for the implementation of the European conventions of Luxembourg and The Hague in 1980 on "recognition and restoration of custody", he conceded that the elaboration of a satisfactory solution to the situation of "displaced" children from Franco-Algerian couples came up against "much more difficult difficulties", notably by its quanti-tative aspect, since "to stick to the official statistics, whose number is naturally lower than the real number", one notes "171 files of

---

42. Catherine Erhel, "Profession : voleur d'enfants", *Libération,* 07-88.
43. Guy-Pierre Cabanel (1927-2016), senator from 1983 to 2001, member of the Radical Valoisien Party.

legitimate children representing 336 children and 54 files of natural children representing 67 children". I am in the "natural children" column. But as a comparison, the senator notes that "on the same date, the number of files with Morocco was 14 and 29 with Tunisia". The problem is Franco-Algerian first.

Algiers, May or June 1988

"I'll stay..."

I am 14 years old. I understand that the moment is important but I am scared to death. I look at my sisters first. Why are they only asking me? What if one of them wants to stay? And then, will we be separated again?

Inside my whole body, it is an infernal chaos. A thousand questions collide, the most insignificant of which will earn me a beating if I say it, since it has to be said to strangers who are not very reassuring and under the control of the artisans of my entire misfortune. With the hindsight of years, an analogy will come to me: I am a tortured prisoner whose torturers bring me for a moment in front of the representatives of a humanitarian organization who ask me if I have been mistreated... *If I answer that I want to leave, do you take me away right away? Is it over right away?* No, of course not. Then I will go home, and Noury will kill me. He's told me a hundred times he'd rather see me dead than surrender to Annie or France. I think: *You don't know them, I will be beaten and probably killed!* If I had the certainty that they would take me away, that a yes would get me behind the desk, with my sisters, untouchable, then I would say that they beat me and what I really risk! Questions of life and death that need to be answered instantly rattle and storm under my ungrown teenage skull. On my

11. The choice? What choice?

shoulders I feel, like clawed talons, the paws of Noury and Mouloud. Then, without my wanting to, I hear myself mumbling a "no, yes, no..." that I hope is inaudible enough so that they won't blame me if it turns out badly, but explicit enough so that they understand that I want to go back. I look at them and think: *Why are you doing this? Can't you see that I am afraid of what will happen in any case? Why are my tormentors present?* Later I will learn that this was the subject of a discussion by the parties involved in the organization of this meeting. The parents lobbied "in order to protect the children".

You bet.

I think I'm asked other questions along the same lines, but I won't remember them. In my mind, everything will be synthesized by this sentence that still resonates:

"Do you want to go home?"

Look at my eyes, you fool, they're screaming yes!

With hindsight, the feeling of my guilt and a few years of analysis, I wondered if I had not unconsciously wanted to send my Algerian family a message with a paradoxical psychoanalytical trigger: *See, I am still here in spite of all that you do to me, so you must be nice to me, I am good and benevolent.* No, probably not, it's twisted, I don't know anymore, but I remember very well the feeling I have when I get up from my chair to come back to the big room: I am physically inhabited by the certainty of having let my only chance pass, or rather that they have stolen my only chance. I have lost, there will be no second try. I want to start the scene again, but there is only one take. One moment I stand up, ready to run to the small room of men in ties, I take a step, Noury looks at me, a new family has just entered. It's over. It's freedom that passes through my fingertips. The life that flies away.

Sitting back in the big room, I am devastated. I wanted them to understand, they didn't. What mistake have I made again? Is it my fault again?

Of the 180 children present, I will know later that 40 have returned, others have obtained visiting rights which will not be respected most of the time.

Before entering the room, Yemma had told me what I was going to be asked. She begged me to say no. She said:

"I'll die if you leave, I'm sick you know.

Noury said:

- You don't want to kill your grandmother?

And then he promised:

- We will arrange things for you, you will be able to take off the veil, we will send you on vacation to France..."

When I came back to the big room, my mother was there. The two families B. and D. are there, Mousse and Mouloud are between me and the press, I must be a special case because many journalists try to approach me, but there is always someone to push them away. I am scared to death. I am afraid of them, I am afraid of the men in ties, I am afraid of the microphones...

I notice a lady who looks at me with kind eyes without asking any question, I look at her lips, without any sound, she draws some words that I read: *It will be alright, children*, I think I understand. I answer in the same way: *We want to go back*. I see her sad and loving face. Noury and Mouloud are behind me, they do not see me. I don't know who this woman is, I will never know. But I have not forgotten her.

Here, I am trained, we leave the hotel, we go up in the car. We return to Annaba. It is finished.

I don't remember saying goodbye to my sisters, maybe I did.

11. The choice? What choice?

On my return, I lock myself in my room. I am aware that I am at a turning point in my life. I believe that I am making the most important decision at this moment: *If I don't commit suicide right away, I must no longer be a victim, I must fight and not let myself be beaten anymore. No longer be a beaten woman but a woman who fights.* I go into the living room, Yemma, Noury, Moufid, Azz are there. I say:

"I have something to tell you: I regret having stayed. But from now on, either I kill myself with sadness, or I fight. I'm going to fight, and you, Noury, the next time you hit me, I'll hit back.

I had never answered before.

- You will hit me, but I will hit you too."

He laughed contemptuously, aware of his strength. As if measuring himself against me makes him feel great. He is a fool.

I go back to my room.

From now on, at every moment of solitude, I only think of the positive memories of France. I put aside, I almost forget, all the misery I lived there. I want to go back, I will go back. I am becoming deaf and blind to the reality here. In a way, it is a radicalization that responds to that of my uncle tutor. I speak very little. I close myself, even to Yemma, but not to Khalid.

Moreover, my grandmother's attitude changes. A few weeks later, she made a nasty move on me, which I forgave her for not suffering more. She decided that I would go on vacation to the home of one of her friends, married to an Oriental man, "until the whole affair was over". She often speaks in Arabic with her sons, but I understand now, even if I say nothing. I understand that they want to hide me, they are afraid that the police will come looking for me again. I ask the question directly, and they tell me that no, everything is fine, but it is suspicious. I tell myself that maybe there was a decision in my favor and they don't want to tell me, maybe they will come to get me to bring me back to France and so they decide to hide me, maybe the ministers or the police saw that I had said no under pressure.

One morning we leave. We drive twenty-four hours without stopping, or almost. I don't know where we are, but I know the geography of Algeria; if we drive twenty-four hours from Algiers, we are in the region of Djanet, Tam, or even Timiaouine, on the border of Mali. We finally stop at the foot of a yellow building, on a sandy street, and climb up to an apartment with peeling walls. Yemma explains to me that I will have to be very good, to clean the apartment every day. I will spend three months there without going out. To get some fresh air, for a few minutes at nightfall, I can only go to the back balcony which overlooks the desert; in front of it, there is another balcony, but I could be seen from the sandy street. I am sure that I am being hidden from now on. Paradoxically, this gives me hope. Even though I spend my days indoors, I am veiled. They check that I do all the prayers. I will understand later that they are fundamentalists. I don't know what that means exactly at this point in my history, but if I see that they behave like Noury, I think they are as crazy as he is. On my birthday, in August, they give me a present that Yemma has reserved for me but I refuse it. In September, I start to get impatient. I tell them that I will miss school. Noury came to pick me up in October, without even a phone call to warn me, or else they didn't tell me. I missed a month of school.

In the summer of 1989, it was even worse. Since my family is rich, I was sent to a very poor acquaintance in Yemma to "learn about poverty". I think to myself that this is really disgusting because if my family is rich, I don't enjoy anything, I just want to get away, so why should I be punished for something I don't enjoy? For a sin I didn't commit? It's quite far from Annaba, in a village. There is only one room, I sleep with the lady. The toilets and the kitchen are shared

11. The choice? What choice?

with several other rooms. It's awful. I think that they are trying to hide me again. I am kidnapped and my kidnappers entrust me to other kidnappers. Where will this mise en abyme of my confinement stop? What will be the next step? Death? It is again a terrible summer. I am storing up so many experiences of hatred that I already perceive that it will take me a lot of time and work to free myself from it one day, if I am given the opportunity. At that time, I reject Arabs, their language, their culture, I vomit them. I feel rationally and humanly anti-racist, but even today I have episodes, puffs of hatred. I have friends who are atheists, Jews, Catholics, Muslims... I have a hard time when their discourse becomes radicalized, I feel deeply that it is toxic for me. I know it's a conventional speech but I am sincerely intolerant to intolerance.

I have veiled friends, converted or not, but I don't have any in chador, that would bother me a lot. In France, on TV, or in the political discourse of the right or the extreme right, everything is mixed up, but the difference between the veil and the chador is at least as great as between the veil and no veil. I do not question their beliefs or their person, but their chador locks me in. Yet, in June 2019, when I went to walk in the boondocks, I felt that they were also my people, albeit differently. And I was able to verify that the Algerian youth was magnificent.

A little before, for the beginning of the revolution of the smile, I also militate, place of the Republic, with numerous and enthu siastic Algerians of France. To leave the dictatorship, to go towards the democracy. But the very vehement speeches at the microphone are detrimental to the cause, they shout, they extremize... It is certainly detrimental to the cause, they are seen as crazy. This attitude provokes rejection, it is not the right method. It immediately leads to polemics, to arguments. Once, I asked the DJ to play songs by the revolutionary singer Raja Mezian[44], beautiful and recent texts, revolutionary songs that could mobilize us all... and all. But I was badly received, sent back to both my identity as a woman and as a non-Algerian, which deprived me of the floor. I was nicknamed "the little French blonde of Repu", which was a way to isolate me and therefore to silence me.

Many Algerians feel an ambivalence, an inner conflict between Frenchness and Algerianness, between religion and atheism. My friend Djamila was so sad that her daughter had a religious wedding with a rapper that she withdrew into herself for six months.

In the bled, they call me "gawriyya[45]", the Frenchwoman, the foreigner. There is a self-hatred in Algeria. Not everyone recognizes it but it is known. Fellag[46] expressed it so well: "We can't stand ourselves, since we kicked you French out, we fight among ourselves! Ah if only you had been a little nicer, there was room for everyone." And to regret the schizophrenic relationship of the two countries: "At the same time we are clandestine when we come to France, and at the same time we can not live without you."

Noury also oppressed me as a French person. He poured his hatred of the colonizing people onto me. Yet, I know that he did not succeed in implanting this hatred in me for good. Friends even tell me, "I don't understand how you can love us." I don't confuse my exasperation

---

44.Author-composer of rap of Berber origin, born in 1988 in Tlemcen. After studying law, she tries to obtain the status of lawyer which is refused by the president of the bar of Algiers because of the subversive texts that she already composes and interprets in parallel to her studies. She left Algeria in 2015 and was welcomed as a refugee in the Czech Republic. She is now considered "the singer of the Hirak", the smile revolution that begins on February 22, 2019 in Algeria.
45.The term designates both the French and the Western foreigner. In Algeria, it has a particularly French connotation. It is also used in a benevolent way, but most often it is an insult.
46.Comic author, actor, director and writer Kabyle Algerian.

11. The choice? What choice?

with hate. I may even have "an ambivalent relationship with my other culture" even though I hate that my co-author says that.

In restaurants, with Arab friends, it happens almost systematically that the waiter addresses me. Sometimes I let it go, but last week, in a restaurant in the Marais, we got up without consulting each other and left. We got up and left! Am I at peace with my two countries? In any case, I don't believe at all in the hierarchy of cultures.

After the 1988 meeting, and despite his promises as a horse salesman, Noury turns up the violence a notch. When he discovered that I had a walkman and tapes, he tore them off and tore up the tapes, then he beat me because music was forbidden to me. Up until that time, beatings were targeted, they were slaps, spankings, belts on the buttocks or legs: that was the punishment. Now, punishments become indiscriminate hand jobs, kicks on the ground, punches; he throws me on the ground, hits my head against the wall or on the ground, strangles me... He puts his strength of man and all his hatred into it.

After 1992 will come the time of revolt.

12.
The ultimate betrayal

"Giving voice to pain: the grief that does not speak whispers to the swollen heart the injunction to break."
William Shakespeare, *Macbeth*.

Paris, 2021

I decided to change my name. This has nothing to do with any desire to escape racism. I fight racism, I don't run away from it. I am blonde, light-eyed, dressed in European style, I don't wear ethnic jewelry very often, so I leave few clues. And this morning, in shorts and a *crop top*, you would have to be Umberto Eco or Philip Marlowe to reduce me to my Algerian origins. Or the director of the business school I just entered... I showed up on time, the reception was good, my diplomas are appropriate, in short, I'm going to get the job and I'm happy because I need to get back on track after my COVID. Everything was fine... until I handed her my passport:

"I'll be back, I'll make the photocopy for the file".

She takes a long time to come back and I understand, as soon as she opens the door, that something has gone wrong. Avenging and determined on the phone and then during the beginning of the interview, she became distant and vague:

"We need to think again, we'll call you. Anyway, we're not sure we're going to recruit yet...

- Really? But you were ten minutes ago!"

At this point, I still don't get it. It clicks when, perplexed, I walk through the door, just after shaking his limp hand. I turn around, I'm a block of anger:

"Is that my name? You saw my Arabic name on my ID card, right?"

She looks down. That's it, yes. I don't know what to do, torn between the desire to throw myself physically on her and the imperative need to move away from this toxic space as soon as possible. I throw myself at her, I stare at her with all the fury in me, twenty centimeters from her face, I say: "Yen3al din rabbkoum[47]!" A few years later, I will read the beautiful book by Hamid Aït-Taleb, who became Xavier Le Clerc, and the anger will come back to me to hear this multi-graduate tell Léa Salamé[48] that by sending the same CV to the same companies he never had an answer with his Arab name when he had a hundred with his French name. In France, in 2022.

I am not the most exposed to racism, but I have had my fill. In 1995, just back in France, I was a cashier at the Félix Potin in Boulogne. I had a hard time keeping to the schedule because I came from Charenton and there was a strike all over the Ile-de-France region[49]. That morning, my last in this supermarket, my cashier manager summons me:

"It's unacceptable to arrive late, you're rude, just like everyone else from where you were born."

47."Damn your gods and religions."
48."La Matinale", September 7, 2022.
49.Strikes of 1995.

I got angry, I was fired, but I left before slamming the door. She is Franco-Portuguese, she was born in Portugal and I in Lyon! I feel like I'm in a Coluche sketch. There is also a lot of discrimination at the university. My classmates did their thesis in six years, I did it in four, they have tenure, I don't yet, they have French or Italian names...

A French name would have helped me, everyone with an Arabic name knows that... but again, this is not my motivation. I want a French name because I don't want to bear the name of my torturers anymore. The procedure is long. So sometimes, when I'm in a good mood, to the question "Civil status?", I answer... : Complicated !

At the university, my Arab identity is an embarrassment, at the place of the Republic, it is my French identity that is an embarrassment... Decidedly, yes, complicated civil status!

Barlu terrace, June 2022

Wait, I have a message from Pearl. I look at my phone: "Still nothing. I'm waiting. But I've decided, I'm going to leave without my sister. When I'm in France, it will be easier to get her back."

Where were we? Ah yes, Grandpa is giving me back my papers. They are out of date, but I have a plan. Pépé also tells me that Annie is in Algeria - "She took over your sisters who were with us" - and asks me if I want to see her.

It was very complicated to find us again because I hardly go out. Grandpa came back every day in one of the stores of the district, as we had imagined: one day at the grocer's, another at the tailor's. Monday here, Tuesday there... so as not to arouse any suspicion. And I was to come as soon as I could. Finally, the conditions are met on the seventh day after our first meeting, Khalid's sister made an order in

12. The ultimate betrayal

a store on purpose so that we justify going there. I find Pepe towards the fitting rooms and he gives me my papers. "As I wish everything to go well, I say goodbye to you", he says to me. In fact, I never saw him again, even if everything did not go well...

At the same time that he gave me back my papers, Pépé gave me the time and place of the appointment with my mother. It is far away, on the other side of the city, and it has become more and more difficult for a single girl to get around, in Annaba or in any other city or village in Algeria. My mother cannot ignore this. Why didn't she give me a closer appointment? Khalid offers to take his father's car with tinted windows, but this is impractical for many reasons, the least convincing being that an unmarried woman goes to jail at the first police check if she is caught in a car with a man. Besides, I don't want him to put himself in danger for me. I'll take the bus. It's an ordeal. I'm glued and groped by all the men around me. I have learned to practice the pinprick trick, which is very well known in the Maghreb. I take a pin out of my veil and I prick the gluers who, in general, do not dare to resist. I wear a full chador. It's practical, I'm less insulted than women who just have a scarf, and I don't risk death, like those who have nothing. The appointment is in a suburban neighborhood, at the end of a dead end. I immediately spot the car with the black windows and the diplomatic plates that allow me not to be bothered too much at the numerous roadblocks. It is the war. I open the back door on the street side. At that moment, I am happy, maybe I even love my mother. In any case, I am hopeful. This is my mother. I remember exactly that maelstrom of feelings that makes me hug her as soon as I sit down; or rather, I try to curl up in hers. I wait for her to close them but she doesn't. So I curl up to force her tenderness. She ends up having a gesture that annihilates me, a little pat on the back, as to a child that one reassures while thinking of something else. It is the panic in my head. I speak first:

"How are you doing?

I should have known better, I've heard this phrase my whole life:

- This is not the time.

It is all the brutality of my childhood that jumps to my throat. I think: *Why didn't you come to get me*? but I am so afraid of the answer... I say:

- How long have you and my sisters been together?

- This is not the time.

Again! Then finally:

- What's up? Grandpa told me you wanted to see me."

The words knock me out. Has she forgotten what she did? Or am I crazy myself? Did I not invent my misfortune? Dreamed it up? I am terrified. I measure at this moment the denial, necessary, in which I lived these last years, idealizing my mother not to sink, associating her mentally with childhood, with France, with the good... to keep me reference points, a hope. I don't want to "see her", I want to escape, to find my life, my stolen childhood. To be reborn. I am stunned by the naturalness of her casualness, it seems like we just saw each other last week. Sensing the tension, she smiles and even becomes voluble, but I soon understand that she is simply trying to know what I know.

"How long have you been seeing Grandpa? What did he tell you?Have you seen him several times?

I answer the truth to everything:

- No, it's by chance, twice, he must have told you, right?"

My answers seem to satisfy her, she frowns again. She still asks if I told anyone about our date. I answer that I haven't, even though I told Khalid and his sister.

"So Grandpa gave you your papers? Do you have them?"

I don't answer; suddenly I am afraid. I think back to the departure from Mauguio, I see Annie again who tells me not to give my papers to anyone... I don't answer. After Pépé gave me back my passport, I looked for a place to hide it. And the safest place seemed to be my underwear. So I sewed pockets in several of my underwear. Of course, I always have them on me, and since I wash my own clothes... The only risk is Noury. Once, he came to grope me while I was wearing one of these panties, I screamed and struggled like never before until Moufid's wife came. I had never fought back before, he was so surprised that he didn't beat me.

At this point, I'm still thinking that the car will start, that my mom will take me. But that doesn't happen.

Are you taking me?" I finally ask in a low voice. But I already know the answer:

- It's too dangerous, there are roadblocks, and you don't want to give your papers...

- But we have diplomatic plates!

- It's not the time, we'll go home and you'll join me in Algiers.

- But how will I get there?

- You figure it out!"

Some things never change. She adds that she has access to the passenger lists and that she will pick me up at the airport when she knows that I have taken a ticket.

Except that I have no money, no phone, no right to fly without my guardian.

I remain silent. Everything tells me to be wary of her. I don't trust her even though I am still very far from having understood everything.

Finally I say:

"My papers are out of date, anyway.

- It's easy to do again, and I work at the embassy!

I pause for a moment. At the embassy? I left Annie idle and unstable in Mauguio and here she is working in a big embassy? I tell myself that the family has helped her[50].

I remain silent. I expect her to yell at me to get me out of the car, but it doesn't happen. I then ask:

"Are you going to take me back or advance me to Noury's because it's far and the trip was dangerous?

- You figure it out, get out of the car."

I go out. I go home on the bus. I feel strange. I think to myself that maybe she's hooked up with my uncle, at the same time I want to believe it. I hope I will leave. My bus arrives just in time in front of the college so that I can meet Khalid and his sister with whom we agreed that they would wait for me until a certain time in case my mother did not take me or if something unexpected happened. They are both happy and sad to see me come back. Khalida is very sad, she understands better than Khalid, and probably me too. A few days later, Khalid takes a ticket in my name. He says that he will accompany me and that he will stay two days in his Algerian apartment so that I can take refuge there if things should turn out badly. At first, I refuse, I don't want to risk his life, but he insists, so I accept. In the evening, while kissing each other, we even dream of leaving both of us if the whole affair goes wrong. It is impossible and we know it, but it feels so good.

When I arrived at the airport in Algiers, my mother was there waiting for me. How did she know my arrival time? My ticket was only taken the day before! Today I still wonder. I go towards her, I know that Khalid watches over me, far away. I am protected. Almost

---

50.To this day I don't know what his exact job was at the French embassy in Algiers. About his hiring, the eighties and nineties were still good years for the French diplomacy and the embassies recruited more easily than today.

12. The ultimate betrayal

happy. Then, I approach my mother and I take her in my arms but, once again, she remains unmoved, the arms along the legs. Yet I feel confident again. I am in Algiers with my mother, my real family. I turn around, I see Khalid in the distance, I make a small wave of the hand that only he can understand.

We get into a cab that drops us off at Telemly's house. It's in the center of town, ten minutes walk from Khalid's house, where I can easily take refuge if things turn out badly. As soon as the door opens, I see my sisters, we embrace, I hold them close to me, they answer me. I can even feel their bodies shaking. Except for the episode in 1988, it has been more than eight years since I last saw them. The embraces are prolonged but Annie intervenes:

"This is not the time for kissing.

We look at each other all three, interloquées…

- Well, yes," says Rose.

Annie asks us to go sit in the living room.

- Let's make pancakes to celebrate, I love pancakes! said Rose again.

I answer that I haven't eaten it for eight years, it was *haram*. I'm fine with that.

- We'll make you an Eiffel Tower of pancakes.

I like the image. But Annie still breaks the mood:

- You're not going to do anything at all, you all sit down."

I suspect that something will happen. My initial enthusiasm is waning. But we do it. I sit in the middle of the couch, my sisters on two nearby chairs, Annie on a chair facing me. My mother takes a hostile tone, well, more hostile:

"I have to explain the situation, you're not on vacation, this is not a party."

To begin with, she forbids me to leave the apartment, in order "not to endanger us". I don't understand why I would put them in danger.

I agree but I feel bad, it would have surprised me not to be still guilty of something...

"Okay, we'll help you if we can, but you're not going to get us into trouble again, because this is all still because of you."

Because of me? My kidnapping is because of me? And the beating of Noury? And the separation from my sisters? I look at her with round eyes. Her mouth pinches, her eyes stare at me, she says, detaching each syllable and pronouncing the final e:

"The letter."

13.
The years of lead

"It is in the name of morality, it is in the name of humanity, that
the worst crimes against humanity have been committed."
Boris Cyrulnik and Tzvetan Todorov, *The Temptation of Good is
Much More Dangerous than that of Evil,*
Éd. de l'Aube, 2017 and 2022.

I listen on the radio to Samia Ammour talking about her youth
in Kabylia during the black decade[51]. Noura is of my time and my
suffering. Her exile is mine. It is to me, to my hands, my eyes, my ears,
to my hatred and my fear that she tells the pestilential neighborhood
of death, the overcoming of fear, the need to take refuge in oneself to
survive, and the uprooting...

In the 1990s, Islamist terror reigned in Algeria. I am not a specialist in international relations, but I know that it did not happen by
chance, that the powerful found their interest in it, and that it is the
people who paid the bill.

51.Samia Ammour : " Mon exil a été forcé ", " Parcours de combattants " produced by
Nassira El Moaddem for France Inter, 03-07-2022.

First there are the "great dead", presidents and artists who fell for great causes and small disputes. There is Mohamed Boudiaf[52], the president of the Algerian High State Committee, assassinated in the center of Annaba. And then the professor Tahar Djaout[53], riddled with bullets in front of his house by the FIS assassins because he was "communist" and "an enemy of Islam", the statement of claim will say. And the poet Youcef Sebti[54], the journalist Smaïl Yefsah[55], the ecologist Salah Djebaïli[56], and the writer Abderrahmane Chergou[57], stabbed dozens of times while shouting "no, no, no..." as a final refusal, and the psychiatrist Moufid Boucebci[58], and the French journalist Olivier Quemener[59]...

One day when I walk in Annaba, I am surprised: from all the stores of the main street go up the accents of the music of Cheb Hasni; I stop a saleswoman and I ask her the reason:

"What? Don't you know, he was just killed downstairs from his house!"

I cried in the street. Journalists are killed very often. The corpses are filmed and the national television shows them every time, to show the barbarity of the terrorists. Sometimes, between broadcasts, we are shown images of the morgue with people whose throats have been slit, so that we are afraid of the terrorists. Sometimes we see people with their throats sewn back together. One evening, I see a

---

52. On June 29, 1992, he was in office since January. Hero of the independence, founding member of the FLN.
53. On May 26, 1993, seriously wounded, he died a few days later. He was 39 years old. He is one of the most famous journalist-writers of the country.
54. Grieved on December 28, 1993. He also taught sociology.
55. October 18, 1993.
56. May 31, 1994, international footballer and researcher.
57. September 28, 1994, Member of the Socialist Vanguard Party.
58. 15 June 1993, he was one of the founders of Algerian psychiatry.
59. February 1, 1994, independent journalist. A prize bearing his name is awarded each year by Reporters Without Borders.

mother with a child on each side, their throats cut and sewn back together. Her belly is open, she is pregnant and the fetus is sewn up. She has a matchbox in her hand. The journalist says that the terrorists are inhuman: "They murdered this family just as the mother was about to make dinner, she still has the matches in her hand." I will see this matchbox for a long time. The terrorists are satisfied because they want us to know what they are doing. Noury has forbidden me to watch TV, but it's okay to watch the killing of miscreants.

The college where I study is often closed. Walled in. It is a university of miscreants. One day, the students decide to occupy the college[60]. I planned to be there, without telling anyone, of course, but the night before the occupation, the terrorists attacked the university residence. They kidnapped dozens of girls, slit the throats of the others... The occupation was cancelled.

And then there were the "big" attacks, killing dozens of people, against a police station in Algiers[61], the Houari-Boumédiène airport[62], a diplomatic residence[63], a consulate... and the hijacking of airplanes, the mass slaughters in villages.

After my departure, in Bentalha, the GIA and the military will assassinate more than four hundred people. The rai singer Cheb Aziz, and the immense Lounès Matoub[64], and the monks of Tibhirine...[65]

The fear is daily and chilling. For me, death at that time has the face of close and beloved friends. That of Yezza, in Annaba, in 1993. With Yezza, we have common courses of mathematics at the university

---

60. A scene of college occupation is very well rendered in the film *Papicha*, by Mounia Meddour.
61. January 30, 1995, 42 dead.
62. August 26, 1992, 9 dead, dozens injured.
63. August 3, 1994 against French personnel in the Aïn Allah city, 5 dead.
64. June 25, 1998, Algerian poet of Kabyle expression.
65. 21 May 1996, 7 dead with throat cut.

13. The years of lead

and, when they do not come to seek me, we return together. Her father is an intellectual, he writes books and is involved in the promotion of the French language in Algeria. This morning, he takes us to another friend's house, next to our old high school - we were in high school together with Yezza but we didn't see each other much; the calculations of Al-Khwarizmi[66] and the douga douga train[67] brought us closer. When her father stops the car, we get out to wait outside. We do not risk anything, we are veiled. Yezza turns her back to her father, who has remained seated at the wheel, I face him, and I also watch for the door of the building from which our friend is going to leave. That's it, she arrives, she smiles. Suddenly, on her left, I see three men appear. They run and push her. She falls. I don't see the machine guns right away. My eyes register the scene of the men rushing towards us without really understanding it. Who are they? What do they want? Are they really heading towards us? Or are they joining someone behind us that I can't see? The only thing my brain can tell for sure is that they are not military. They don't have uniforms but long jellabas. And they are masked. I remember that I want to scream but no sound comes out of my mouth. They are less than a meter away from the car, my friend's father looks up. He turns his head towards us. Yezza turns around at the same time. She screams. I watch her father's head explode as three guns fire continuously for seconds that are hours. The square is empty. One of the men throws us to the ground with his fists. We fall on top of each other. I am on top. In the distance, I look at our friend huddled in the corner of the porch of her building. An old Mazda approaches. The three men start shooting again, in the air, as if to prevent any attempt to intervene by passers-by, who are far away

---

66.Arab mathematician (780-850). He classified algorithms. He is also called the "father of algebra".
67.See Chapter 16.

anyway. By the time they get into the car, the silence becomes total. Deafening. I see Yezza again at her father's funeral, she doesn't stop shouting. I will try to go and see her afterwards. But they tell me that she doesn't want to see anyone, that she doesn't speak anymore, and that she has become crazy.

At that time, many women, especially young ones, were kidnapped. Sometimes they are not found, sometimes they are found abandoned, dead, in a dump or on the edge of a rock, sometimes they come back, the terrorists throw them back alive in the street or in front of their houses, but it is almost worse because they have suffered a thousand torments and, for this obtuse patriarchal society, the worst of them, rape, they are discarded. From time to time, we hear that one of them came back pregnant, therefore guilty, another one scarred... In 1992, a close friend was kidnapped. She is a student, young, atheist. It is a dangerous way of militating. She disappears for several weeks. And one day she is thrown out of a car in front of her house. They kept her for six to eight months. Then they got tired. She was already crazy when she came back. Her parents threw her out on the street. She committed suicide. In Beausejour, on the one hand, our neighbors are foreigners, Germans, I think, who left in the early nineties. But on the other side lives the M. family, whom I've known since I've lived here. I am friends with Rachida and Fatima, the older girls. We went to school together. We don't see each other as much since university because we are in different cycles; above all, our parents don't see each other anymore since Noury's radicalization, which cut us off from many other friends; but I still go to their house from time to time, well, when I have permission... Before the events, I also liked to take care of Rachida's and Fatima's little sister. This year, she must be 5 years old. Sometimes I also liked to borrow a book from the library of my friends' father, who is a professor of philosophy at the university, even if I couldn't bring it home. He told me one day that "the problem with Islam is that it has only one book, it is not enough to awaken the critical spirit, it needs several". "Critical thinking"... the expression strikes me, I will make it a rule of life. Our gardens are adjoining and there is a communication door between the two. One morning, I noticed that the door was wide open, although it had always been closed since the war. I looked over and saw the big door of the house on the terrace, flapping in the wind. I approach it and enter the hall. I see red stains on the floor, it's blood. The stains are round with a jagged edge. This strikes me because I have had enough nosebleeds after Noury's hand jobs to recognize that the blood has fallen in large drops, like when one cuts oneself and holds one's hand high, or like from a bleeding nose. On the left, the two doors of the living room yawn, I have the presentiment of the drama at the moment when I discover it. My two friends lie on the floor. Their throats have been slit. Fatima holds her throat with both hands, as if to bring the two lips closer to the deadly cut. A little further on, their father is also there. His neck has also been cut, but so deep that his head is detached from his body. I don't know how long I remained petrified in front of these dismembered bodies. Images went through my head: the weather is nice, we are going to school, the father is smoking his pipe in a big club chair, the mother is preparing a snack for us... I don't scream. At least I don't remember it, but I leave the house backwards. Then, arrived at the door of the terrace, I start to run towards the door of the garden then to the kitchen of our house. I find Naadi, Moufid's wife. I try to speak. I am in a sweat. It takes about 15 minutes for me to calm down and explain the situation. I describe the scene of horror that I discovered, I say why the open door intrigued me, I try to make my anguish understood... But suddenly Naadi interrupts me to ask the question that I should have thought of right away:

"Have you seen the little one?

I replay the sequence in front of my eyes: the door, the terrace, Fatima, Rachida, their father, the blood... where is the little sister?

- And the mother?", adds Naadi.

We rush again towards the house. I don't want to go there but Naadi pushes me, she gives me courage, even if I see that she is also afraid. Arrived in the living room, we call slowly; in the panic I forgot the name of the small one, it is Naadi who gives it back to me by calling it to me in a muffled voice:

"Salma, Salma..."

No answer, we call louder, we shout, we search all the rooms, the floor. I end up finding it. She is buried under the bed of the parents, in the farthest angle. Astonished, she will say to us that she remained very a long time without making noise. It is Fatima who told her to hide there. On the bed, there is her mother, with her throat cut.

The massacre of my friends remains a nightmare in my head even today. Noury says that it is normal, they were miscreants and their father used to work at the prefecture, that's why they were killed. He was retired but that doesn't matter. Noury says that we are safe if we are with him, and as long as he doesn't decide to kill us himself. He has the power.

Today, when I try to tell my friends or family about those years, I can see the disbelief, I can read in the eyes of my interlocutors the "you are exaggerating".

Fortunately, on the radio, Noura says the same thing I do. She tells of her friends who were murdered in front of her, of the permanent fear, the paranoia, even, that settles in the families.

The two dangers of Algeria at that time are the fundamentalists and the police. Almost at equal level. Advantage to the madmen of Allah, though. Of these, Noury is supposed to protect us, since he is part of their gang. But it's not that simple. There are groups, power games. I think Noury is in the upper echelons, but since he killed a man in front of the mosque, he has not hidden his concern. The man's friends have him in their sights, and Noury is not sure he can count on his own "friends. And then there are the police. When Noury was first arrested, I know he was beaten. At home, conflicts often break out between Noury and his brothers. The atmosphere is heavy. Everyone suspects everyone else. Myself included. After Yemma's death, I overhear a dialogue between Haya and the poor old woman to whom Yemma had sent me on a summer "vacation. I hear:

"If you don't continue what your mother Yemma was doing, the child will wake up. I was the one doing the prep work, I brought you what you need for a month, I'll bring you the rest later."

Here I must make an aside. The border between belief and superstition, between the sacred and the evil, is narrow and porous in religious societies. And the Algeria of the nineties is a society in full rediscovery of its religiosity. In the D.'s, we are educated and rich, but the house and the speeches are full of chicken feet and conjurations of the evil eye. Hypersensitivity to chance, or rather to its impossibility, which supposes that an evil hand acts in its place, and therefore that destiny commands. Everything is written. Nothing very different from the great Catholic cinema of Bresson or Rohmer, for example... except that in the daily Maghrebian incarnations of belief, one finds potions, formulas, imprecations... and the discourse that I hear does not shock me. I have integrated the idea that one can, by stratagems or liquors, act in secret on the psyche of an individual. For example, when Haya's husband cheated on her, it was not said that he was a cowardly, lying runt, but that his mistress had bewitched him. Either way, the woman was guilty. Terrorists and Islamists were also said to have been the object of a spell. Witchcraft, the evil eye, even in a very religious society, has weight. When my uncle Moufid had huge abscesses, it was also said that he had eaten a poisoned rat, for example - it is often the rat that is accused. Doing witchcraft was sinful, but it was everywhere.

So, in revolt, I burst into the room shouting:

"You want to poison me to force me to stay but your drug doesn't work since I've always wanted to go back, you'll never be able to take my mind."

But in 1990, I got a stomach ulcer and made the connection. I convince myself that my food is contaminated with dead rats - a familiar threat - or spices that I am made to ingest. I say I won't eat at home anymore, a hard promise to keep. Later, I tried to understand: What was I being given? What preparations was this crazy old woman talking about? Was Yemma trying to subdue my reason with the chemistry of potions? Had I been dreaming the whole episode? In the most brutal adversity, in spite of the most violent sufferings, the heaviest bruises inflicted to my body, in the heart of my misfortune and even in the full consciousness of preferring to give myself up to death, I never felt that my spirit was dominated.

14.
The letter

"She has already forgotten. She will swear on her crowned head that I am making it up. This crazy imagination, destined to destroy her own, she won't ask where I got it, she knows it. [...] She will say that I lie about everything. But that doesn't matter, I'm the one who writes."

Maria Pourchet, *All the women but one*, Pauvert, 2018.

Paris, May 24, 2022

Tonight was the first public gathering of the Enfantiste collective[68] who invited me to present the cause and the association of EVRP. We met in front of the City Hall at 6pm. I was contacted by Claire, the day before:

"We are in a bit of an emergency, but would you be willing to speak on behalf of the abducted children?

- Obviously, this is the core of my life, it's all I do."

So I spoke in my name and in the name of the association. No one can really speak for the abducted children, no one but themselves,

---

68. The collective Enfantiste, created by Claire in 2022, gathers different associations against any violence made to children.

and the road is so long to free this word... It is essential for them to understand that they are not alone. Others are experiencing what they are experiencing, feeling the same betrayals, hoping for the same liberation.

When I returned from Algiers to Annaba, after the 1988 meeting, my solitude was terrible. I was hidden, removed from possible research. I was isolated. But it was too late. I had regained hope and understood that other children were living my ordeal. That's when I decided that one day I would write this testimony. The first step is often, always, to fight guilt. It is the first hill to climb, but it is an absurd, Sisyphean mountain. Often, I think I have climbed it, and then a detail, a memory, a discussion, brings me back to the foot of my Everest. A detail? A memory? A discussion? For me, it's a letter that keeps making me lose my balance. A cursed letter, the key to my history, a burning abscess around which the ball of my tormentors is organized and the tour of my misfortune[69].

Algiers, July 1993

"The letter," she said again in the same tone.

The words have been echoing in me for thirty years: "The letter". I had to expect it. Responsible and guilty. But of what, in the end? Damn it! What have I done that deserves to be rejected again when I come back from hell?

I look at her amazed and sad...

"But you know very well that I was forced to write this letter, or if you don't know, you can at least understand it when I tell you!

69.Joseph Kessel is one of my favorite authors, especially his great work, *Le Tour du malheur*.

I know she doesn't want to understand. I know it's pointless, so why am I arguing? I retreat, I let my guard down.

- There's no need to take your poor victim's face, we know what you are like, anyway I have no intention of getting you back after all the evil you've done. You never think about others, you never think about me!"

There, it is said, she will not take me back. She says the last words while screaming. My sisters approach me. They hug my waist without me knowing if they are embracing me or holding me. There is so much tension. I feel that they love me but also that they want peace. For my part, I am ready to do anything to get back to my family, especially to leave Algeria and the yoke of Noury. Noury is now accusing me of having broken up with the D family.

"They could have helped me, they are rich, but now they hate me, it's because of you!"

She is completely incoherent, I realize that it is pure hatred that expresses itself through her mouth, and that reasoning has no place there. Since Noury forced me, as soon as I "arrived" at their house, to write this letter, she should admit that I did not have to "convince" them to hate her! And then, they don't hate her, I don't think so, she just doesn't count for them, but I can't say that. I tell her that she could come to see me, that the door was not closed, Yemma always said so! She came only once and it was already to tell me that everything that happened was my fault! But nothing happened:

"With the letter and with everything you said in France, the DDASS and all that, I was stripped of my parental rights. That's why I could only get your sisters back by breaking them out."

It's not true, I know because Pepe told me about it, about this "escape": my mother was very theatrical when she came to get my sisters, but "it was her," said Pepe, "who entrusted them to us and she knew that she could come and get them whenever she wanted, there was no need to play all this comedy, she even alerted the neighbor that she was coming to "make her children escape", while we were waiting for her on the doorstep with the little ones' bags, we were just surprised that she would show up after all these years.

I wrote the letter just after Annie's only visit to the D's in September 1985. When she came at that time, she had not forfeited her parental rights, as she claims, so she could have taken me.

"Why didn't you do it, then?

She stops, stammers... I catch it on the fly:

- I couldn't... DFS... not the time.

It's never the time with her. And what does the DDASS episode have to do with it?

- The DDASS is in France. In Algeria, that doesn't count, you could have taken me and instead you left me saying that it was my fault and that they had bought me.

My sisters intervene:

- Please, let's make pancakes!

But Annie is on a roll. She describes her life today, so that I understand that I don't belong there:

- I'm with Younous now, and I hope you won't ruin my life with him like you did with Beny in France.

It's true, I always rejected her lover Beny, but, deep down, it was because she was betraying Mouloud and that didn't fit in with the ideas of justice and honesty that they were trying to teach me at school. A few decades later, on a personal pilgrimage to Mauguio, I will see this Beny again, he will apologize. And so will I. Annie returns to Younous:

- I'm going to marry him as soon as we get back to France.

She said "we", that's all I can remember. Am I included in this "we"? She calms down:

- Your sisters are minors, they can't go out without their father's permission, you are not allowed to leave Algeria. We could go to Morocco, with our contacts in the police, but there are conditions for you.

Once again, she leaves the idea that she will take me along, but if there is a condition, I suspect that it announces more suffering for me. And then to go out by Morocco... it seems to me that it is all made up, but I say nothing, I wait for the continuation. Again, she asked for my papers. As she works at the French embassy, she is able to make me a new passport from the old one. This is even how it is usually done, I know, but I am afraid. I'm torn. Anyway, the next move comes along and completely removes me from the doubt I am in:

"Younous has a friend in the police, we told him about you, he saw photos, he wants you. And since he is in a high position, it will be easier to get out of the country.

I am knocked out. She quietly tells me that she has promised me to the chief of Younous. All of a sudden, the anger chokes me. I remember the scenes in the chapel of Mauguio. I think back to Noury's hands on me, I see again Yemma's duplicity in explaining to me that she cannot oppose my marriage with the warrior from Afghanistan... I am angry but... I collapse in tears on the sofa. She adds:

"That's the contract, I'll give you three days to think about it."

And then, I think about it, how could they show him pictures of me when they haven't seen me for eight years? This is the proof that they had contact with Yemma and Noury, only the D. could have sent them pictures of me! No matter which way I turn, I only encounter deception and betrayal. The terrorists and the policemen are the two scourges of Algeria at that time, the two responsible for the war, why is it necessary moreover that it is to one then to the other that I was successively promised? And then, anyway :

"I want to marry whoever I want.

Annie relents:

- But don't worry, it's a ploy, once we're in France, you can divorce..."

For me, nothing is more important at this time than getting out of Algeria. I could even accept a marriage if I had a chance to escape afterwards. But I have the conviction that she is tricking me. She will escape with my sisters and leave me in Algeria with this man. She's not trying to get us all to leave, she's sold me out. We have to gain time:

"In fact, I am like my sisters, a minor for life, since everyone decides for me.

Save time again:

- The D.'s are powerful, I will be reported to the border.

And most importantly:

- Noury is my guardian, in Algeria it is he who decides for me, it is he who gives the authorization to leave the territory and the authorization of marriage!

And then, if we stay in Algeria, I could never divorce or even return to France. If we're in France, he won't want to divorce me either for a long time because he couldn't stay in France. In short, this whole thing is a trap.

- What's in it for him? Why marry me if he's going to divorce me afterwards? I asked Annie.

His answer froze me:

- But you're so stupid! You'll find out about his interest after the wedding!

I wrote the letter while crying under the dictation of Noury and Mouloud, who came from Algiers. They told me:

"You have to write about how you lived in France.

I wrote that I loved my sisters, and then school, my classmates, the piano... but it didn't fit.

- No, you have to write down what your mother did to you.

And Mouloud practically starts dictating the letter to me, stopping every now and then to ask me questions: Was I eating enough? Were there many people coming by the house? And then the drugs drying in the hallway, the alcohol... I knew right away that it was a trap, but I wanted to believe it, so I asked them:

- If I write all this, can I go back to France?

- Yes," said Noury.

- What if I don't write?

- If you don't write, there will be this." A huge slap lands on my left cheek and sends me tumbling against the wall. I sit back down and write. What else can I do? I am 10 years old, my mother abandons me, men beat me and I am dictated a letter. I write.

And after all, what did I write that was so scandalous?" I said to Annie defiantly. Didn't you strangle me every morning in the shower? Didn't I get arrested by the police? Didn't you force me to participate in an orgy? Weren't there drugs drying all over the house? What did I say? The truth, and that's it," I challenged him.

She is distressed but soon comes to her senses:

- It's all in your head, you wrote it to hurt me, you're bad.

It makes me angry because Noury uses the same phrase "it's in your head", these are damaged, distorted memories...

I am furious but I give in.

- I don't care about all this, I can't take it anymore, I want to come back, I want to go back, I want to be with my sisters, in the house in Mauguio!

Turn the page. To find my life again. To be reborn even.

- Ah, but here is my little crybaby again, the little innocent, lying, hypocritical one...

Then she adds:

- You have three days to accept the offer, the terms of the contract.

My sisters are in tears.

- Think about it and enjoy your sisters because if you say no in three days, that's it, you won't see them anymore. On the third day, I'll come home from my job at the embassy and you'll give me an answer; if you don't agree, I'll put your uncles and the cops on your ass."

I say I'll think about it. I am serious. She leaves me, my sisters follow her. I fall on the couch. I fall asleep but I don't know how long. When I wake up, it's getting dark outside. Annie and my sisters are in front of me. Annie says:

"Your sisters have something to tell you.

Rose signals that she doesn't want to talk. I encourage her. She nods and sends me a kiss. She was so smart. Fleur speaks, forced by my mother:

- You go ahead!

She gets up in a state of shock, she almost screams:

- It's your fault, you don't realize how much you've hurt mom and us, it's all your fault.

I say tearfully:

- You don't know, we'll talk later, you have to grow up...

My little sister says:

- Well, now we can make pancakes?

My mother gives me a nasty look and adds:

- But yes, of course, what do you want your little mother to make for you? Dumplings? You used to love them."

I say yes, nodding my head. But my sisters insist on pancakes. So first I have dumplings, then pancakes for dessert. I eat like crazy. In the middle of the meal, Annie disappears. I only see her again in the evening, when she comes home accompanied by her new fiancé, Younous, the policeman. He does not look at me with malice but I am wary. She explains to him in front of me that she is waiting for my answer for the wedding. Younous says:

"Tonight we're eating on the big balcony."

There are three balconies in the apartment, the large one is the dining room balcony. After dinner, I go to isolate myself on the small balcony of the bedroom. Younous comes. I feel that he wants to be friendly, but not me. It was him who "promised" me to his boss. We got to know each other anyway. Besides, he takes the opportunity to explain me "the plan". He is voluble, makes gestures, goes back ten times, smiles all the time, I feel that he wants to convince and reassure me. But in the end, the *deal* was clear: I had to get married in order to go to France. I pretend to hesitate, but my decision is already made. I have to leave. Their plan is rotten, they know it, they only want to get rid of me, one way or another, and if it can serve their interest, it's even better.

In the evening, my sisters put mattresses in the living room so we could sleep together. We lay down and talked a lot, then we fell asleep and fell asleep, embraced. I have a vivid memory of waking up with one sister in my arms and the other on my stomach.

I had the best night of my life.

15.
On the street in the middle of a war

"One expects only sorrows, dead-end roads.
One acclimates, in short."
Horace Engdahl, *The Cigarette and Nothingness*,
Serge Safran ed. 2014.

One of the voices that has helped me rebuild, and even just survive these past few years, is Boris Cyrulnik. I owe him so much! I have read all his books and listen to him every time he comes around. Even if I know that the concept is nowadays overused, and even recuperated by capitalism and advertising, I give to resilience - with which he has familiarized me - a very personal meaning: it is the capacity to intellectualize over time my revolt, my absolute insubordination, from the dramatic events that have marked my past, events that I arrange as I can in order to build the story of my life. Doesn't he himself say somewhere that one "always invents one's past"? So I invent my past. This does not mean that I only take from it what interests me, suits me or comforts me, but that I reconstruct it through the prism of my present, with the cognitive biases of my current life. I look for keys in Algeria and behind Noury's blows and Annie's betrayals that will open a path for me, I look for hope, a reason to live, and this quest naturally transfigures the meaning or importance of this or that episode. Was Yemma sincere or manipulative, or a bit of both? Did Noury love me? And Mouloud? And Annie? And my father? In the complex sfumato of my existence, the same clues can lead to opposite conclusions. How can I find my way through? No doubt, as Cyrulnik says, by putting together "bricks of truth" that will end up building and reconstructing "the chimera of my life.

Algiers, July 1993

The day after this beautiful night, the countdown has already begun. My mother and Younous left early for work. We didn't see them. But there is a note on the mirror in the entrance. Annie insists that I don't leave the apartment. And neither are my sisters, of course. I stroll around in an old tee-shirt nicked from Fleur. My sister wants to make pancakes again, but we have neither flour nor eggs. We turn on the TV, more images of the attack. But I find a French channel. I haven't seen French television for eight years. I greedily devour a magnificent TV shopping show where enthusiastic housewives acquire unforgettable clothes brushes in a maelstrom of sonorous occlusives and vibrant nasals. The voice of Pierre Bellemare, who reigns over this small television market, enchants me. I close my eyes. He takes me to France. Then we watch "Hélène et les garçons". My sisters tell me that they are fans. I discover this soap opera that I find a little childish, but their pleasure in front of this small and sweet series touches me. Later, in Paris, when I will happily go into my fifties, I will never miss an episode of the sequel of the series. "Hèlene et les garçons" brings me delightfully back to my sisters. But reality catches up with me. The ultimatum is running out. And Khalid is leaving in a few hours. Should I run to join him or stay and enjoy the three days Annie and Younous have set before I make my decision. I stay. And I decide to take my sisters for a walk, despite the ban. However, I must see Khalid before he returns to Annaba. I know that Mousse, Mouloud's brother, also lives in the neighborhood, and I am afraid to meet him. But we arrive without difficulty at the foot of Khalid's building. I ask my sisters to wait for me in the hall, which is a safe place, and I go upstairs. Nobody answers, so Khalid has already left. Yet I had one hour left. We slowly retrace our steps. I am pensive. At the corner of the street of "our house", Fleur asks me permission to buy sweets in a small store where they have their habits, on the other side of the street. I keep Rose in my hand and we go to sit on a small bench that we had just passed. I watch our house from the bridge. There is a strange activity in the entrance and on the street. Men come and go, waving their arms. Shouts come to us. Hypervigilance is a built-in part of my being now, and I often worry about nothing, but there is danger here, for sure. Suddenly, on the opposite sidewalk, we see Fleur, she has come out of the store, has not seen us and is running towards our house, towards the danger. A car appears from nowhere and stops with a long squeal of tires at her height. Two men get out and grab my sister. I yelled, "Fleur! One of the men turns around: it is Younous. I am both relieved and scared to death. Why is he there? He will surely kill me for not having respected my commitment and for having put my sisters in real danger.

The car makes a U-turn, it comes towards us. Younous and his colleague make us get on board quickly. But we don't go towards the house, we go towards the embassy where Annie works. Behind us, gunshots are heard. Younous says:

"We got an alert at the station, terrorists are in the neighborhood, I just had time to jump in the car to come get you.

15. On the street in the middle of a war

To me, in Arabic, he said:

\- I told you not to go out!

Then relents:

\- ... but you were right to come out anyway because, to escape from the neighborhood, the terrorists went through our balcony.

Behind us, the sound of machine guns goes up another notch. Terrorists? In our house? Did Noury send someone after me? Are they Islamists? Is this a set-up? Isn't Younous just trying to scare us by taking advantage of a quarrel in the street? I ask him the question and answer him in Arabic. He smiles:

\- Believe me, I'd rather.

Then adds:

\- Trust me, by the way we won't tell Annie, we won't say you went out, I'll explain it to your sisters."

That's fine with me.

So we go to the embassy and we park for a few minutes while waiting for Annie to join us. Then we go back. The neighborhood is quiet. The incident is over. Annie doesn't ask any questions. My sisters say they want to go eat at Wang's, the Chinese place where the family has its habits. It is at Maqam al Chahid. The atmosphere is relaxed, I smile, Annie too. The egg rolls are delicious. But suddenly, a man approaches. He is visibly drunk and provokes Younous: "Considering your ugly face, having two blondes is a lot", he says, staring at Annie and me successively. Younous gets up and takes him to the street. We follow him, panicked. Younous is furious, he beats the guy on the sidewalk with a violence that reminds me of Noury, then lifts him up and handcuffs him to a post. His nose is bleeding continuously. He spits blood too. The girls are petrified. Annie tries to reassure them. Younous pushes us towards the car. At home, an argument breaks out. We reproach him for his violence, and even his cruelty, because, with the curfew, there are strong chances that the poor guy is picked up by a patrol and will rot in jail for a while.

Younous keeps a low profile and goes to bed. The next day, when we wake up, he tells us that he has gone to untie him, the "poor guy". Impossible to know if he is telling the truth, but what is sure is that we can die if we do not respect the curfew.

"We don't have to live like this," I say to Annie as she prepares to leave for the embassy. She looks at me with an evil smile:

- You're not in France, this is how it is!"

As if I didn't know. Finally, being with the police is as dangerous as being with the terrorists. I left a family and a guardian who is a terrorist who is a target for a family with a police officer who is a target.

The day is spent in front of the television but I do not find the enchantment of yesterday. I am already tired of Bellemare. With Fleur, we do not talk about her accusation again, but the uneasiness is there. In the evening, we have dinner at home and we sleep together again with my sisters. The next day, Younous comes back before Annie and tells us to do the laundry of her clothes. I think: *I'm not your maid, you jerk,* but obviously I'm keeping this to myself. Annie comes in just as I'm hanging out the laundry. She jumps on me:

"You've just arrived and you're already circling him, you're being a maid, aren't you?

I reply violently:

- You're an idiot, I don't care about your boyfriend, of course I didn't think that for a moment, he asked me to do it. If you had known me better in the last few years, you would know that I have a lover, but for eight years you haven't asked about me and you treat me like a stranger."

She calms down, and the evening passes quietly, even if everyone (except my sisters who did not understand all the consequences of

15. On the street in the middle of a war

the "deal") pretends. We fall asleep again in the living room. And in the morning, it is the third day. Before leaving for work, Annie addresses me:

"If you stayed, it means that you accept the marriage, tomorrow you will be presented your husband."

I don't answer. I know they are both going home at 5pm, with Younous picking up Annie at the embassy. I won't be there when they return. In the afternoon, we cook with my sisters. As we are peeling carrots and potatoes, I say:

"I have to go get the bread, Annie asked me to.

I kiss my two loves and I take my small bag. The little one looks at me, kisses me again and says:

- I have a feeling the bread will take a long time to bake."

I know she understands, but I don't let anything show, especially not to create a situation that could compromise them and put them in danger. And I don't want them to fight because of what Fleur told me the other night, for example.

As I close the door behind which I am sure Fleur and Rose are crying, I have absolutely no idea where to go or what to do. So I walk in Algiers. I wander, rather. I have the distinct impression, and almost the desire, that my death is near and inevitable. It is coming. It sees me. It touches me already. In the moment, the feeling is undoubtedly more metaphysical than palpable, but I have also thought about it *afterwards*. And the result is clear: I have no chance of survival. If my uncle finds me, he kills me; if terrorists find me, they kill me; if the police find me... My existence has no way out. I am lost, panicked. Most of all, I am tired, so I look for a stairwell to rest in. I will have plenty of time to die tomorrow! Most of them are closed and even barricaded. It's been like that in Algiers, Annaba or elsewhere, since the beginning of the war. But I finally find one. I went upstairs. On the fifth and last floor, I push open a door, it is a small room without light. Brooms and crates are stored there, like in an attic or a big closet. They won't come looking for me there. At least not tonight.

Above my head, I see a trap door, it must lead to the roof since my little home is on the top floor. I will come back in 2019 in this place, to see, to remember, to find myself lurking in this cold and dark room, and maybe measure the distance I have come. For two days I don't move. I am afraid. But I am also thirsty and hungry and I have to resolve to go and satisfy my physiological needs in the street. I find a dead end where I can relieve myself. Then a shopkeeper offers me some fruits, I find some bread in a garbage can, drinking is more complicated because the tap water is not drinkable but I end up finding an old lady at a window, who offers me a tea. I drink almost a liter. I have to go back urgently to my dead end. Anyway, the street is dangerous... I absolutely need help. The police is the first idea that would come to the mind of an American or a Swiss, but it is the last for a young girl without money or papers in Algeria in 1993. The idea came to me as I was walking back to my shed. As I walk slowly, I am jostled by two men who laugh and talk loudly. Thrown against a wall, I rub my forehead while cursing and I close my eyes as if to control the sudden pain... When I open them again, I see a lawyer's plate! There, I need a lawyer, better, a female lawyer, a westernized woman, to be confident. I look at the signs along the streets in the district where I am, it is a middle-class district. I select about twenty of them. Tomorrow morning, I will start ringing doorbells. For the moment, I return to my building with a thousand years of fatigue and a tiny basket of dates. I am about to push open the door when I discover on my right a copper plate with the magic words: *Law firm, fourth floor*! Just below "my place!" There are two names. The first one is known, it is a big family, they surely know the D.; I choose the second one which

15. On the street in the middle of a war

seems more common: B.Betty I go up the stairs quickly, I knock, a woman opens, she is dressed in western style and she smokes.

Before she's done saying hello, I'm spouting off like crazy:

"Are you Mrs. Betty?

- Yes.

She has a cigarette in her hand, which gives me confidence:

- I need help, please, but I have no money, and if you call the police I will die.

She brings me in and sits me down, asks me if I'm thirsty, brings me water, and then tells me that I probably need to call social services for my case. I thought so.

- I don't have any money, so you're not interested in me..., I said, holding back tears.

- Okay, sit down, get well. When you are ready, you will calmly give me a little summary of your life before you end up in the attic of my building.

I try. The kidnapping, Algeria, Noury, the escape, my mother... After a few minutes, I think she has understood the essential. I faint. When I wake up, another woman, older, is leaning over me. "That's my mother," says the lawyer behind me. She has a Hayek on her head. I eat a little more, then fall asleep on the couch where they have put me. When I wake up, they explain that they were going away for the weekend - but what day is it?- and suggest me to accompany them to rest. I feel like my life is changing. How long has it been since I've met a caring, selfless person? Someone who wants to help me, or just wants to consider it, rather than beat me up or marry me! They put me in a car. We pass two roadblocks. It is dangerous. Especially if it's a woman driving, and there are three of us.

We arrive in a beautiful house surrounded by trees. The neighbors are far, it is the countryside. A shepherd passes with goats. I calculated that we are about one hour from Algiers. There is a terrace, armchairs, a barbecue, it looks like a vacation home. These women are rich… The mother prepares us food. And the lawyer explains the plan to me.

"I believe you when you say you are in danger, we have to think, I know your family, I know the power of Noury.

This does not make me feel better, but she relents:

- We shower and eat," she says happily.

After a good dinner, Betty installs me in a big armchair on the terrace and starts to speak with her mother. They talk about me but they don't address me. This does not bother me, on the contrary, I find it a sign of interest.

Our ultimate goal is to send it to France," says Betty.

- So she needs to have her papers in order," adds her mother.

I straighten up and unbutton my jeans in front of the two inter-loqued women:

- I have my expired French papers and an Algerian ID card in my pants."

They laugh. They tell me that a great French writer, in her youth, used to keep the licorice she stole from the grocery store in the same place, and years later justified it by saying, "What do you want, it's the only place where we wouldn't go to get them[70]. We all laughed. I think that, for me, the risk is still there, but I don't say it, so as not to break the small moment of light joy that we share. Betty says, "It will take time. She evokes the possibility that I find a job in the meantime, I am old enough to find a job now, it would be a way to gain a form of independence before leaving; as if she was thinking out loud, the mother says:

"She might even work for us at home or in the office.

70.Annie Ernaux, *The Empty Cupboards.*

15. On the street in the middle of a war

Betty dismisses the hypothesis:

- It would complicate everything."

I don't see how, but I trust him. We decide, after a delicious tea, that we will talk about all this again the next morning. Indeed, in the morning, we find ourselves again on the terrace. Betty confirms me that they are going to make everything to help me.

"But you're from a family we don't mess with.

This was true before terrorism, it is true during it, it will be true after. The bourgeoisie renews itself but it does not die.

- And we don't have much time," says the mother.

Several times during the day, while I am busy reading, making bouquets - the garden is full of wildflowers - and eating gazelle horns, I overhear the two women talking to each other in low voices. I don't get the impression that they are trying to hide from me, but rather that they are looking for the right way to tell me something. In the evening, the verdict is in:

"We're going to negotiate with your uncle to get you back "home".

I'm already crying.

- Don't worry, it's temporary, but if you stay here, we'll get into trouble, they can press charges, and everything will become more difficult.

Betty adds that as a lawyer she is able to get some kind of agreement from Noury that I will be treated well.

- That he will not kill me? I asked.

- Yes," she stammered, "and we'll make sure, I'll call regularly with a code set up between us to check on you."

I'll stay with them for a few days and when I feel ready, I'll go home. In the meantime, she's going to call a judge to see if anything can be done about my papers. But the next day, the judge says that we can't do anything. There is a ban on leaving the country and there is no question of contesting it. He is afraid, too. The following morning, Betty calls Noury, that lasts a little, but I understand with the smile of my friend that we have gained cause: Noury commits himself not to kill me, that reassures me a little. He also agreed that the lawyer would call me regularly, every day at first, then at non-fixed times. He also agreed to withdraw the complaint he had filed for "kidnapping" - he was not lying, the judge had confirmed that there was also a wanted notice for runaway or kidnapping. So I stay a few more days, rest, then one morning I say:

"Okay, I'm ready to go back to hell."

She gets me a plane ticket. She tells me that as soon as I have papers, she will help me. And not to hesitate to come back to find her. In total, I will have spent ten days of happiness with my new friends. That's already a lot.

I remember my arrival in Annaba. I am at a window seat. Suddenly, murmurs go up, they are passengers who are alerted. A black smoke escapes from the port wing. The stewardesses try to calm down the passengers. The captain makes an announcement to explain that we have a small leak, but nothing alarming, no worries. I hope that the plane will fall.

16.
Noury killed me

> "A spark will extinguish my soul
> Leaving life and dying
> Buried in a black hole
> Where the man
> Nothing will be remembered"
> Farid Meghari, *Le Mendiant du bonheur*, Éd. Tafat, Alger, 2014.

"It was because of turbulence." I've been saying one word for another a lot since I did that long COVID. *Turbulation* for turbulence, for example. I'm naming things wrong.

COVID over three months long, from the beginning of March to June 21. My brain was in a thick fog. It's getting better but I'm still in slow motion. And that's on top of my post-traumatic condition and seizures.

I had students returning from Wuhan, I understood that the health crisis was serious. At that time, in early 2020, I was teaching at the École des ponts and at Sciences Po. It leaves a metallic taste in my mouth. And I smell burning everywhere. Even today.

Sky of Algiers, August 1993

So the incident was not so harmless and there were many reasons to worry despite the reassuring recommendation of the captain since we turned back. The smoke on the wing was the beginning of a fire, due to a "turbulence". I see it as a sign of destiny. I must not return to Annaba.

However, I'm coming back on the next flight.

It was Azz who picked me up at the airport. I was a little surprised. Azz is the third in descending order of siblings. He is very busy with the family business and generally doesn't care about me. He and Noury get along well in business, although his brother despises his choice of marrying a former prostitute. Noury has made several death threats against him and "his Red Head whore[71]". Azz is an atheist, I will learn long afterwards, I think he did not talk about it at the time, especially in front of Noury. Still, I find it strange that Noury would send me someone he doesn't really trust. For a moment, the idea crossed my mind that Noury wanted to "give" me to Azz. I don't know why. Maybe it's a way of reminding me of my place in the family. To entrust me to the most discredited of my uncles, a way of telling me that I am a lesser being thrown to a lesser being. But Noury is not so smart. Or too impulsive for that. His violent passions always take over. In fact, that's part of the punishment. It will take me years to understand it, but Noury is a child, so he sends me the message that he's sulking, as if it would make me happy if he came... I ask where we're going.

"At Noury's. He is your tutor, he is like your father.

I ask that we stop to buy a veil. If I present myself like that in front of Noury, he will hit me. He answers:

71.Quarter of the prostitutes in Annaba. See also chapter 5.

- Don't imagine for a moment that I'm on your side, I won't do you that favor."

I should have had the lawyer give me one! What an idiot! We're coming home.

As soon as I cross the threshold of the house, Noury takes me under his arm in a falsely affectionate gesture. He holds me tightly and draws me to him. My head is down. Completely at his mercy, I feel deeply the situation of domination. Slowly, he approaches his head to mine:

"So, did you have a good time?How is Annie doing?

I was counting on him not knowing what I did! Even today I wonder if he spoke to find out or if he was informed by the Bs. I deny it because I don't want to put my sisters at risk. I panic. I defend myself badly:

- I was in the home of some women who took me in, she is a lawyer but I rang her doorbell at random, I wasn't looking for a lawyer...

I don't know if he doesn't believe me or if he doesn't care. He doesn't care, I think, as if it didn't matter what I did. Like it doesn't matter anymore.

- Come on, let's go to the garden.

He pushes me, there are stacks of books placed at the entrance of the garden:

- What? Do we have to bury books?" I said, suspicious.

It was the worst episode of my life. But I think it is also the one where I resisted the best. I have always felt, even today, moments where I feel like I am stepping out of my body to watch myself live from the outside. I look at what is happening to me from above, as if it were happening to someone else. There is a psychological explanation, it is typical of post-traumas. When the pain is too strong, one leaves his body, that makes it possible to resist more easily because the events which occur seem then to concern somebody else, precisely. Otherwise one dies.

When he forces me to get up from my "grave", I am still insolent:

"So we don't bury the books?

He shouts:

- Bitch!", and the first slap fell.

I move my arms and legs to express my will to defend myself, not to be passive, to touch him perhaps, to scratch him, but my gestures turn in the void. The blows rain down. I feel a cheekbone bursting, blood spurting, my eye closes under a punch. He drags me by the hair inside the house. We pass Noura and Azz. I see the fear on their faces but I try to smile and wave to show them that I don't care about the blows. Suddenly a slap like a club falls on my already bloody cheekbone. I fly, my head hits the staircase. He massacres me. I lose consciousness.

Yemma is dead. Noura shows me, from time to time, a form of humanity, but it is a meager, calculated, measured, self-interested humanity... However, I take what there is to take. I know she is distraught. She too is afraid, yet she tries to intervene: "Stop, you're going to kill her! Noury pushes me into the room with his feet. I am like a bloody wreck on the carpet. I see him closing my shutters. I lose consciousness again. When I wake up, I hear thumping outside. He is nailing boards against the window of my room, located on the first floor. I think that I am a prisoner but that *even if I had the strength to want to, I would not be able to escape for a long time.* It is total darkness in my room. A few hours pass. I manage to climb onto my bed. My sheets are red. My blood flows from my cheeks, from my mouth. I have big blue and red marks on my chest and thighs. Noura brings me food. She also puts a bucket in a corner "for the toilet". The days pass. From time to time, once a week in fact but I will quickly lose track of time, she brings me the phone and I have to call the lawyer to tell her that "everything is fine". Each time, as with the 1988 meeting, I have the impulse to scream, "No, I'm locked up, I'm going to die...", but each time, the instinct for self-preservation prevails: if I tell the lawyer, I know I'll be dead before I can finish my sentence. Then I will learn that I have been locked up for more than four months.

One day I wake up in the hospital, I don't know how it happened. I am blind. Little by little, memories come back to me: my room, the bucket, the darkness[72], Noura's little trays... I want to die. I can't kill myself. There was nothing in the room, neither knife nor rope. One evening, Noura even removed the sheets, I only have a big blanket made of raw wool with ears of straw in it. It was psychological torture after the physical torture. I decide not to eat anymore. I throw Noura's trays into the bucket but she doesn't empty it anymore. I spill them from the bed where she puts them, but soon I don't have the strength anymore. I die.

I am blind but I hear the doctor say:

"We're going to keep her on a drip."

He's talking to Noury, I'm sure. I was taken away because Noura came into the room and I wasn't waking up. Noury was not there. He would have let me die. Noura decided to call the ambulance. A few days later, the doctor asked me:

"Why did you do this?

- Do what?

- Why did you try to kill yourself?"

I say I only stopped eating, I didn't want to kill myself. I really wanted to die but I refuse to tell him. I'm still afraid. Of everything.

72.This episode created a recurring symptom in me. For years, I locked myself in my room for hours, sometimes days, in the dark. It was only when I moved to my last home that this symptom suddenly disappeared. I don't know why.

16. Noury killed me

I stayed in the hospital for three weeks. When I get home, Noury corners me on the stairs and says:

"You're a pain in the ass, we had to tell the hospital that you're sick and couldn't eat anymore so that there would be no investigation and the doctors wouldn't get alarmed; if you do it again, you're dead."

It sets new rules. I can go around the house and garden. But I am not allowed to go out in the street. I decided to keep my nose clean. After a few weeks, I asked to go back to college. He says no. I wonder what my life will be like now. Then one morning he walks into my room and says:

"Get ready, we're going to college."

He never took me before. It was always a driver who took me to Khalida's house or to the train. I usually take the niqab off at college. The first few days that I can go back, I keep it on because he tells me that he is making me watch:

"You're going to go back to college but don't be a smartass, I have eyes everywhere."

For a long time the university was walled up. One could not enter it, the Islamists had condemned it. Then some courageous students made holes in the walls and we went through anyway. The university is in the Sidi Amar district. To come from the house, it takes an hour. Most of the time, a driver takes me there. But on free days, I take the train which is called douga douga because of its slowness and the repetitive noise of its machine. They say TDD to make fun of it: it's the great era of the TGV and you can see it everywhere in the magazines I can read at the university. The train leaves from the station, just behind the port.

This is the time of the last eighteen months that I will spend there. After the interlude of peace in the hospital, Noury soon sent me back to the mosque as well. Sometimes I also have to go to the "great dignitaries", friends of Noury who give me some kind of private sermons. I have a great fear of being alone in a closed room with a man, especially a friend of Noury. But strangely enough, none of them rape me. He has even sent me to the homes of female scholars, the few women who have a say in religion. At the mosque, on Fridays, the men are downstairs, the women upstairs, on the balcony. On other days, it's the same, but there are fewer people, so the men downstairs form small groups, each with a scholar or imam in the middle. Women may preach as men. There can also be groups of women upstairs. Or one can follow the rounds of the men below from above. But we don't mix.

Noury also resumes the jihad propaganda video sessions from Afghanistan. I have to use it as inspiration in my daily life, "to take it as an example," he repeats. We watch three or four a day. It takes us about two hours in total. Inside, there are the anachid[73], these repetitive and violent musics which, thirty years later, still attack me when they appear unexpectedly from an open window, a noise from the street or a TV on, like intrusions of an unheard of power in my deep being.

I lost a year because I couldn't study.

In 1988, during the meeting, I saw other abducted children. Two of them, a boy and a girl, I have forgotten their Arabic names but they are called André and Anne, are geographically close. Before 1988, we saw each other at school, but I didn't know that they were in the same situation as me. They stayed through the same silly process as me. They didn't "dare" to leave, for fear of what would happen, because of the same hands on shoulders. We see each other episodically in the train that brings us back from college, or along the concrete rise, at

---

73.Originally, the word means "song" but at that time, in Algeria, it refers to the religious invocations of terrorists.

the bottom of our neighborhood. Our meetings are brief, but always intense, we know, without needing to explain, what we share. André decides one day to play the fool. It's desperation. I don't know what he expects from this behavior, maybe he is really crazy. With us he doesn't seem to be, but as soon as someone else is present he says and does anything. But this avoids him to follow the religious precepts of his father who is also radicalized. In 1992, André committed suicide. Or his father killed him. I don't know. He wanted to send him to join the maquis and the terrorists "to teach him". André told us that he was afraid. It was probably a suicide, because his family maintained a lot of mystery and discretion around his death. If his "father" had killed him, he would have bragged about it and Noury would have told us. We try to hide suicides in families. It's *haram.*

Her family was conservative but not fundamentalist - at the time, of course, I didn't make these distinctions, but I still reasoned in degrees of freedom, in religious constraints... She had a lover like me, but her family decided to marry her after discovering her love. One day when we are alone, we talk about it and we understand that we have the same intention. We even decide to "wait" for each other, if the circumstances arise, to commit suicide together. She also tells me that she has made a *deal* with her lover but she doesn't tell me more. On the day of the wedding, they are presented on the balcony, she makes a sign in a direction and receives a gunshot: it is her lover who killed her. I don't know if he killed himself afterwards, but I think so. Sometimes we thought of killing our torturers, but it was dangerous and complicated, and then it was like behaving like them. Suicide is simpler, apparently... My friend died on the day of her forced marriage. For our generation, a forced marriage is not a "tradition" anchored in the history of families to ensure some transmission, descent or heritage... A forced marriage is a group, a family, a community, which forces a woman to marry whom she does not want. It is a sexual aggression decided and organized by several people against a woman, therefore a collective rape, even if it is physically executed by one person. My friend escaped them.

The end of my studies is still far away, but Noury threatens to anticipate my marriage. So I put all my energy into preparing my escape.

It is 1994, I am 19 years old. Since I return to the university, I see Khalid again. I leave dressed in a chador and then I only take off my scarf, to be able to disguise myself again at the slightest alert, to become invisible again. I got back in touch with the lawyer. Little by little, Noury's attention slackens a little. I start to see friends again. I try to return to Khalida's house. I keep to myself. I look for the limits of my prison, in fact. What I can and can't do. My plan is to get papers, then money for a ticket and… take off as soon as possible after. Money is the easiest thing, Khalid and Khalida can help me. Stupidly, I tell myself that they could bribe customs officers to let me get on the plane. The lawyer tells me that she will know who is on duty at the airport and that we could try to buy them…

In any case, you have to start with the papers. In 1994, the French consulate in Annaba reopened.

17.
The beautiful

"To run away, to get out of it, to extract oneself from the places of decay. To get out of it. The destination is not known but we know what we are doing, we know what we want to escape."
Claire Marin, *Être à sa place*, Éd. de l'Observatoire, 2022.

In 2021, a reporter asked me why I had never been to the embassy before? To ask this question was to not really understand the context. Before I was old enough to go to college, I couldn't move. It's not an image, I couldn't leave the house alone. I was going to high school but it was a couple of hundred yards from our door. I didn't have any money and I was, moreover, very closely supervised. The question still haunts me. Of course, I'm overlooking the cutishness, and even the obliviousness of the question... as if it were that simple. But still: has my whole being always been tense towards the sole objective of escape? Wasn't there a part of me that was accommodated, albeit temporarily, to my "new life"? The answer is yes, to both questions. As I said, some abducted children are so disconnected from their original environment at such an early stage that managing their return becomes even more complex and delicate. I even hear from researchers and lawyers that no return is desirable, especially if it is seemingly not desired by the child. For me, I had the "chance" to be abducted when I was 10 years old... but a part of me was "accommodated", another part was patient, another part, even bigger, was afraid... And a part of me loved a part of this stolen life. Because one does not live anywhere between the ages of 10 and 20 without friends or support... And then there is the comparison with my life before Algeria, the argument repeated a thousand times about the misery of my life before, the blows of Annie, the possibility of prostitution, drugs, death... A large part of my life before Algeria was terrible, I am aware of it, but, beyond the fact that the second one made me regret the first one, who could arrogate the right to impose another one on me? Even beautiful and rich, my life in Algeria would have remained based on a crime, a kidnapping of which everyone, Annie, Mouloud, Noury, Yemma... is guilty at some point in my story, at some point in my history.

But I had to live. So I never accepted Noury, of course, but I sometimes tried to make myself accept him. I understood early on the duplicity of Yemma, but she loved me, in a way, and a part of me loved her. The same for Moufid. And as the devil is in the shades, I loved and still love Khalid, and he returned that love, but not always as much as he could or should have. My story is also a story of calculated loves and of hands not far enough or not long enough held out. The lawyer in Algiers helped me, but she also sent me back to the man who tried to kill me. My aunt Alice, Mousse, Kima, girlfriends and sometimes shrinks... everyone has commented on my suffering. So few people believed me until the end and with constancy! This is the main reason for this book. This zone of lost possibilities and missed escapes that this journalist evokes, it exists. With more determination and a bit of luck, I could have escaped from hell sooner. But between saying it and doing it, there is the need to escape and the ambiguity of life, there are the three dinars missing to take a bus, the aches and pains that make you give up the idea of going out, there is the fear of being hit, the lack of self-confidence, the temptation to give up and the tears of the fate that persists.

My beloved sister even accused me. That's why this man's question, cuistre and brutal, has always been with me... like a kind of metaphysical "what if": "What if" I had had more courage, "what if" I had kicked harder with my feet in the door of the car that was taking me to the Joliette... Finally, there are the "what ifs" that determinist philosophers attach to ineluctable fate, and Kieslowski[74], on the contrary, to a cascade of small - and often bad - choices. "What if the customs officer in Marseille had listened to me, what if my Aunt Alice had protected me better, what if my mother had died in the van accident, what if the lawyer had kept me with her, what if the social services had done their job, what if, what if, what if... Damn, in the end!

The chance meeting (Kieslowski again) with Pépé was the material trigger. To recover papers was to find an identity. My journalist, on the other hand, sees this from his window, he only perceives the sequence of events and the cold logic of the intellectual answers that must be given. But when I want to be kind to myself, which happens more and more - it's a good sign, according to my shrinks and Olivier - I see myself veiled, threatened with death, without money, surrounded by hatred, I say to myself that it is understandable that my judgment is somewhat impaired, that I ride on chimeras or that I miss the obvious.

One day when I was thinking about how to get out of it, for example, I understood that the embassy had no reason to believe me

---

74. Notably in *Le hasard*, 1987, then in the trilogy *Trois couleurs, Bleu, Blanc, Rouge*, 1993, 1994.

17. The beautiful

when I said I was French. Of course, they have the means to verify it, but if they don't, only I know. And then the line is the first obstacle, the guard the second, the offices the third, the documents, the fact that my mother works at the embassy, the threats... these are some of the additional obstacles I could point out to my pragmatic journalist.

My story is gone.

Oh dear, my co-author is going to be angry with me again, but I forgot to mention that during my wandering days in Algiers, before finding the lawyer, I went to the French embassy. It was a Wednesday at 5 p.m., to avoid Annie who was coming home early that day, and to keep the line short - I learned the ploy by chance when I overheard an exchange in Arabic between Noury and Yemma about Algerians trying to flee the country: around 4:30 p.m., the embassy guards start sending people away, but if you insist, explain that it's urgent, they sometimes let people wait, and there are far fewer people; the lines are monstrous for visas, less so for other procedures... Annie often has contemptuous words for people who come for a visa. So I knock on the door and immediately tell the guard:

"I'm not here for a visa!

I show my expired passport, he opens it:

- I'm here to do my papers.

- It's too late, he replies.

I insist:

- I just want to see someone.

My goal is to get into the office. He calls a lady, I think it's a secretary, I explain that I have to redo my papers, and I tell my whole story in a few sentences... I didn't say my mother's name but they ask me:

- But then, your mother must be looking for you, maybe your name is in our file of abducted children cases?

I say my name.

- Oh, it's you, Annie's daughter! It's because of you, all this mess ? You made a big mess when your mother only wanted to help you !

I hold back my rage, she resumes:

- Here we can't help you anymore, because of everything you did...

But what did I do wrong in the end? I say:

- My relationship with my mother is private, right? I still have the right to redo my papers, right?"

She says yes and gives me a pass to cut the line next time. I have to come back with a birth certificate. I ask how I can get it, since I sleep outside, it's wartime, we're in a country that's violent with women, and I'm not veiled anymore... I ask for help. Maybe they can even keep me here, as a kind of asylum? (Here, my journalist would say that I am not very rational and I would agree) In fact: "You are Algerian, on Algerian territory!" Would it have been easier if I had only been French? Of course not, but that's what I'm led to believe. I've heard the half and half all my life. Do I have to cut myself in two? I say again that I risk dying.

I don't know what Annie's job was at the embassy. Maybe cleaning or cafes, maybe secretary, she didn't even have her high school diploma. She always blamed me for not being able to study because of me. I left the embassy in despair. I had put all my hopes on it.

Back in Annaba, Khalid and Khalida cheer me up, we work on the plan of my escape. I need a birth certificate. If it wasn't written on the papers that Grandpa gave me back, I wouldn't even know where I was born. I only know that it's in Lyon but I'm not even sure and I don't have an address... I don't write French very well, I've often been taken out of school and in Algeria I didn't learn French very well because it was badly taught to me, and I hardly know how to spell... I write a letter with all my known data, name, first name, date of birth... and passport number, and I send it to the town hall of

Lyon 69004. That's all. I put Khalida's address (would my journalist have found it more coherent if I had sent the certificate directly to the embassy? No doubt, but I wanted to hold the document in my hand, it's irrational but unavoidable), she will go every day to pick up the mail at their house of Beauséjour on the heights of Annaba. Two months later, as we were going to college, she put in front of me a letter with the letterhead of the city hall of Lyon. I frantically opened it and I was disappointed. They ask for details and photocopies of my papers. I curse myself for having forgotten such obvious details. The same evening, I write again. But the good thing is that the letterhead includes a phone number... which we call the same day. Answering machine, voicemail, call back... we finally get them and after two different offices I finally have someone who listens to me. I summarize my situation - I'm used to it by now - and my interlocutor, very understanding, assures me, "I understand, we'll be quick." I ask how many extracts can be delivered, answer: three. Very well, I want three. And I ask that they be sent in three different envelopes to be sure to get at least one back. Ingeniously (my reporter would certainly have said "stupidly"), I conclude by saying, "I'll refund the stamps." This went on for five months. It could have taken five minutes at the embassy. But eventually we get the extracts. All three. At the same time, at the end of March 1994, European consulates reopened in Oran, Constantine and Annaba. This is good news. Obviously, Algerians rush to apply for visas, but, thanks to my pass obtained in Algiers, I manage to enter the consulate in Annaba. I met the social worker, Françoise M., on March 23; I remember her because she was available and kind. She gave me a second pass, valid for the day of my choice, stipulating that I could come to the consulate at any time. The identity documents are only issued at the embassy, not at the consulate, but she agrees to take care of the formalities. I get excited, I've never been so close to running away. I give her a photocopy of my birth certificate, my expired passport (I'm a little reluctant, but I trust her) and I fill out my application on the spot. She sends the papers to the embassy. I come back the following week but it is much too early.

Come back in three months, not before," says Françoise.

I'm scared because it's summer, wedding season, I explain to my new friend:

- If I am forcibly married, I will kill myself."

My passport will arrive in March 1995, one year later. During these long months, I come regularly to the news. Françoise is a kind of psychological support when I despair. And then, on March 15, 1995, she welcomes me with a big smile and these words which still resound in my head: "It arrived. I explode with joy. And immediately afterwards I burst into tears. I am happy and scared at the same time. My passport was ready, but I had to go to Algiers to get it. I can't wait. It's almost superstition, but I'm afraid that my passport will go back. So my idea is to rush to Algiers, get my passport and take off the same day. But that's the idea... "on paper".

Since I gave away my expired passport, the small pockets of my panties can accommodate my embassy passes, but I find it increasingly difficult to protect myself. Noury's touching is more and more frequent. I let it happen but I always keep one arm along my belly, on the side of the pocket, and the opposite hand in protection. He can rape me, but if he finds those papers I am dead. I sometimes say that I have my period, that stops him immediately, but it's an excuse that I can't use very often. Since I am not allowed to lock myself in the bathroom, I use stratagems to wash my panties when he is not there, or I use Yemma's bathroom, where no one ever comes, and where you won't hear the hairdryer.

These months of waiting are also an opportunity to save a little money to buy my plane ticket to Algiers and then the one to France. But not enough, because the price is very high: about 1.5 million dinars, according to the weeks, that is to say the equivalent of 1 500 euros. I manage to do some housework when I get out of college, hiding from my family, but it is very difficult to free up time. Khalid "lends" me the rest, and I manage to go to Algiers. When I arrived at the embassy, I was very happy. Françoise, the social worker, is waiting for me. She surprised me by coming and that moved me, I know that she wants to make sure that everything goes well. They give me the passport. I feel like someone who has been entrusted with a treasure and is afraid of ruining everything by losing it. To the person who gives it to me, I say, "I'm leaving tomorrow. They explain to me that I need a passport and an exit visa, this is the Algerian rule when "a French passport is made for the first time as an adult in a foreign embassy."

I don't understand it, but Françoise agrees: "It's the law.

I have to go back to Annaba, and get an Algerian passport now! In theory, I have the right to do so since I am Algerian, but it's knocking me out. Every time I think I am close to my goal, something unpleasant happens. I have the impression that a dark force wants to prevent me from returning to France. I wonder if my family is spying on me, if I have not been followed to the embassy, if Noury's men are not going to jump on me to confiscate my precious document. I am becoming paranoid.

In October 1994, my mother and my sisters returned to France, I found out from the lawyer, whom I sometimes manage to reach from the Taxiphone store, near the university. She also informed me a few weeks later that the lifting of my ban on leaving the country had not been extended. I can therefore "theoretically" leave the Algerian territory, provided that I have proper papers. I wonder what happened to my sisters? How come they came back without any problems? They probably didn't have exit visas or even Algerian passports. What about me? Do I have one? I searched the house, but I couldn't find a passport in my name. I will have to establish it. And I also need to earn the money for a new plane ticket because the previous one has expired and I have no way to get reimbursed because I need a bank account. At home, there is a room where I am not allowed to go but I know that they hide cash there. Sometimes a lot. One day Yemma told me that it was "family business". I'm sure it's dirty money, otherwise it would be in the bank. But I don't care. I'll take it there, if I can. Rihane, a friend from college, is also going to help me because she now works at the prefecture. She tells me that no Algerian passport has been issued in my name but that with my simple Algerian identity card and a photocopy of my French passport, it will be quick, she promises. I don't believe it but I provide the documents. I am wrong, one week later I have my Algerian passport.

Rihane finds me private lessons. I give some but it is not easy to justify my absences.

And then one day, I will buy the ticket. There, my rational journalist would still have a lot to say... I go to the Air Algérie agency in Annaba. It's an imprudence, everyone knows everyone, I should have gone to Algiers. I am afraid to show my French passport. I'm veiled, they don't expect me to have a French passport, they could confiscate it. It's 1995, there are terrorists and police everywhere. Once again, I had the impression that the employee was looking at me the wrong way, but in the end it went well. I manage to buy a ticket. Everything is stupid, I should have bought it in Algiers. I also had to buy a ticket to Algiers. I warn the lawyer. The idea is to sleep at her place, to go to the embassy the next morning and to take off the same evening. I have planned well because Air Algérie might still be late. In fact, the plane is delayed and we arrive after the curfew. I take a cab. By arriving at the bottom of her house, I am questioned by young people, bearded, I understand at once that there is a danger. If I stop, they will take me away. I am afraid to lose everything but I know what to do: I pass at a good distance without fleeing their glances but by inclining immediately the head to show my respect. I see the lawyer on her balcony who is watching the scene, petrified. They let me pass. I rush into the building. I climb the floors and fall into her arms. One does not sleep too much. I call Khalid. I say that it is okay. We said goodbye to each other in Annaba. It was moving but I was happy to leave. Betty accompanies me to the embassy. I made on purpose to keep my veil to show them how I am dressed from morning to evening. I remove it in front of the embassy employees. I want to show my pain. I also went to see Françoise, the social worker, before leaving. She pointed out that I don't have my repatriate status. But she said that this would not prevent me from passing. I was still worried about it. She said that I would have to get it back in France. She gives me a list of homes. I saved about 1,000 francs in dinars; Khalid had gone to change the money on the street for me. At the embassy, Betty stayed in the car. The guard looks at me strangely with my full dress; in the office, I say that I come to take my exit visa.

"Ah, but it takes time, it's not done like that!"

I can't take it anymore, I shout that I take off the same evening, I come out with a tourist visa. After leaving the embassy, I don't remember anything until the plane. Well, at the airport, it seems to me that the customs officer looked at me with envy, like: "How lucky you are to go to France", but maybe also with hatred. On the plane, I'm on the window side, next to a lady who I find very suspicious, but maybe it's paranoia on my part. I can't believe that in a moment the plane will take off and I will be free. I listen to the announcements in French, the heavy door is closed, I see through the window the ladder of cuts going away... then coming back, accompanied by the screaming sirens of a police car. The door opens. My heart is in my head and it beats a thousand times an hour. My neighbor looks at me:

"You, you're weird."

I don't answer. Two policemen look at me from a distance, they approach, lean over... the front row of seats and a man, probably small, whom I could not see in front of me, hidden by the seat, and check his identity. The man gets up and follows them. You can see the fear on his face. I am relieved. The plane finally takes off. I fall asleep looking at the sea above Algiers. When I wake up, there is still the sea and a shoreline, but "it's Marseille," my neighbor says. Nothing can happen to me anymore.

Paris. I had promised myself to kiss the ground, it's ridiculous, I don't realize it. I am yelled at. We join the bus, my neighbor comes to me and says:

"You, you saved yourself huh?"

I like that she uses the word "save". I say yes. She asks me if I want some money, I think she is sincere but I am afraid to accept. I am afraid of everything. I don't know where to go. I have no memory of customs. I am just alone in the middle of the big hall of Orly, lost, desperately happy. I am finally in France, at home. I take a cab to an address provided by Françoise.

I look everywhere.

18.
Lifetime reconstruction

"Until justice is done to me and to others,
I will be the little girl of this village,
kidnapped, beaten, raped."
Nadia Mourad, from the biographical film *On our shoulders*,
by Alexandria Bombach, 2018.

When I arrived at Orly, I was lost. Françoise M. gave me the address and phone number of an association "but anyway, they will wait for you at the airport". I don't see anyone, but I don't care, I'm floating. I take the RER and get help. At Saint-Michel, I scrape my ribs and my hip by bumping into the blue doors. I emerge into the open air. I look at Notre-Dame. It doesn't make much sense but I fill my lungs with air, like someone about to dive, or to fill up with fresh air. I do this several times. Then I walk on the quays, like an automaton, slowly but without stopping. I look at the cars, the buildings, the people. It's the end of spring, it's cool, especially since I didn't take a coat. I listen to the breathing of Paris. On the Seine, boats pass by, I greet the tourists who answer me. I smile unexpectedly at the people I meet, I open the books of the bookshops. In front of the Louvre, I remembered an article I had read in college that mentioned the construction of the pyramids, I saw them "in real life"; at the Pont des Arts, I crossed the Institut, the rue Bonaparte, Saint-Germain, the bookshops, the statue of Danton, everything amazed me! Until the evening, I don't think for a moment about the rest of my life.

I just enjoy being here. Free.

At nightfall, I am hungry and I buy a pancake and a bottle of water. I retrace my steps, I think: *Paris is not so big*, I find the deep quays of Saint-Michel, I am tired. I see a group of young people with dogs, I settle at a good distance, far enough so that it is not suspicious, and close enough so that they can intervene if I am attacked. They come towards me. They are friendly. I answer their questions but I don't add to them. The next day, they will help me to find the association I am supposed to contact, but for the time being, we enjoy pizzas while drinking beer (water for me, I have never drunk alcohol yet, it will come!) and listening to guitar. It looks like paradise. In the morning, we find the address, it is a home. I will stay there for a few weeks, then I will go to another one. It was in Vaujours. They put me in a room with three other girls. I found it wonderful. I thought everything was great, even the shared bathrooms that smelled of bleach. I will see a social worker who will ask me:

"What is your project?"

No idea, live free. At the bakery of the city, I consulted the small advertisement board, they were looking for a baby-sitter, a math teacher and... an employee at the bakery! I offered myself. A few days later, I was a baker; besides, I had a lot of experience, I had kneaded bread for years at the D.'s! Later I became a cashier, then a saleswoman for pest control products in Evry, then a baker's helper again (in the evening, I left with cakes that had not been sold!), then a cleaning lady. The days passed, then the weeks. At the center, I borrowed books. A world opened up to me, that of culture: reading, listening, watching, intellectually gorging myself on everything I had no access to for ten years. I became a devourer of French literature, art, cinema... This hunger is still insatiable today. It is born from having been deprived of it, I am sure.

Little by little, an idea began to take hold of me: I wanted to go back to school, finally to university, to resume my studies. But there were many pitfalls, first of all I had to validate my Algerian baccalaureate. "Impossible", said a social worker who made me lose several years and forced me to go back to Algeria to get the official document of my diploma, before I could finally register at the Inalco[75]. I will obtain my diploma, I will do a thesis and I will succeed in my university "reintegration".

Less than three months after my return to France, my beloved sister died, murdered by a drunk driver, and I had the impression that I was also dying[76]. I never had the opportunity to speak with her again about the accusations she had thrown in my face and which had burned me like acid, since I never saw her again. But I know from my other sister Rose that she regretted them as soon as the door closed on me leaving. That warmed my heart.

Since 1995, my life path has climbed steeply. Hill after hill, pass after pass, I had to face an abusive husband, a divorce, studies without money, sleepless nights, then the precariousness of my teaching job... and illness, diseases, then confinement, an ordeal for me, so much so that I made up false authorizations to go walking for hours in Paris. Each step was a struggle: renting a room, then an apartment, going through my interviews, presenting myself for the first time in

---

75. INALCO: National Institute of Oriental Languages and Civilizations, formerly called "Langues orientales" or "Langues'O".
76. On the day of her funeral, Annie told us that "the best years of her life were spent with Beny..." while my sisters and I were being taken back to Algeria.

front of my students (what a beautiful day!). And then I became so passionate about Paris, about France. I caught up with my gaps in history, geography and Parisian bistros! And I marched for Charlie and the Bataclan, yelled with Nuits Debout and the Gilets jaunes, cried at France's World Cup victories and Mélenchon's presidential defeats. I hoped in 2019 to finally get a tenure, and then not (but it will come, I believe).

I have been abroad (in Egypt from 2004 to 2009, every year for my thesis; in Tunisia in 2001 and 2003 for two-month stays at the university), meeting people, travelling... I have moved, changed shrinks...

Above all, there was Laure, the light of my life.

A thousand times I was afraid of missing everything. A thousand times I was afraid of losing everything. But I held on. On the other hand, my heart is pathetic. And I'm not even talking about my relationship with sex, well, let's talk about it:

"Do you realize that there are words I learned in 2019 at the same time I was learning the basic sexual acts they designate?", I said one day to a friend, while having lunch at the terrace of a bar on the Canal Saint-Martin. I said it too loud, everyone turned to me and I blushed. I said it, it took me years to formalize the idea that I had been raped tens, hundreds of times. Upon re-reading the chapter on Noury's touching, my co-author had written "fellatio" and "masturbation." I removed them. I'm putting them back in because I want them in there anyway, because in ten or twenty years, I don't want to reread myself and think I should have written more clearly that my guardian was forcing me through these acts, that he was raping me. I'm putting them back here... but it's an effort.

In Edith Bruck's lovely book, *Le Pain perdu*, the author asks herself, upon returning from the death camps where she did not die, why she consistently makes the wrong choices. Why, like me, does she fall in love with a bastard who cheats and beats her? Why, like me, does it seem to her that others go their way when she remains mired in her pain? Why does she give herself to a brutal sailor? Why does she let an unwanted engagement come? Self-contempt? Self-flagellation? Unconsciousness ? Inextinguishable lack of love? These are the questions that psychologists, my introspection, my association and this book help me to answer.

When I created the association, many of my friends rolled their eyes... A close friend even told me:

"No, still your stuff, but don't you understand that you need to move on, forget about...?

I responded very angrily - it's rare that I get really angry with my friends:

- To forget... Where to start, then? What to forget first? A ten year old kidnapping? My mother strangling me in the shower and handing me over to men? My friends having their throats slit? What to forget first? That I was buried alive? That I was kicked by men in a circle around me? That I was locked up for four months in the dark with almost no food? What would you rather I forget first, huh?"

I don't see this friend anymore. We don't forget anything and that's good. Since 1995, my reconstruction has not been linear and I know that one does not forget and it is so much better. I want to heal[77], to heal myself, to repair, I want to feed myself with my life before, to share it, but above all not to forget.

The association I created wants to help children and build a future for them, but it is also a crutch that supports my step. In her beautiful

---

77. In the beautiful film already mentioned, *Incest, Saying it and Hearing it,* the actress Corinne Masiero says about healing: "You don't heal from it but you learn to deal with it, it's like cutting off your leg, you don't heal but you learn to deal with it." I don't think I "heal" either but I want to learn to walk with my leg off!

18. Lifetime reconstruction

film on the reparation of the victims of an attack in Paris[78], Alice Winocour shows how the victims look for themselves like magnets. They return to the scene. They recognize each other, they talk to each other, they are accomplices or guardians of a knowledge, of a feeling rather. The final image is magnificent, when Virginie Efira and Amadou Mbow see each other from afar and their eyes recognize each other without the slightest doubt, they who have never seen each other, flattened victims in a darkened room, who have held hands during a massacre.

Am I getting better? Is hell behind me? No one would understand if I answered no to this question, but I want to repeat the absence of consideration, the non-existence, basically, of the victims... "I don't know, I'm in the middle of a service, right now...", replies a waiter to Virginie Efira who returns to the scene of her pain and asks some questions.I do not know, I am in the middle of a service, there...", answers a waiter to Virginie Efira who returns to the scene of his pain and asks a few questions. Our society does not have time for suffering that lasts. It gives three days for a mourning, and then? And then what? Move on? Of course not. Just as "mourning" only makes sense if it means integrating the dead into our lives, "remaking my life" only makes sense if it means repairing my being. I like the image of the house being broken into[79]. If, all these years, my body and my life had been a house, then burglars would have entered it to steal, break, plunder, take what there was to take. In 1995, those burglars got out of the house, and I have been cleaning it up ever since. I won't replace everything that's broken, but the house is there because I'm alive, so I tidy up, I tinker, I patch up. And it stands up.

78.*Revoir Paris*, 2022, Alice Winocour. Performers : Virginie Efira, Benoît Magimel, Grégoire Colin.

79.I think it came from a phone call to SOS Amitiés in 1999. Thank you for this.

We do not accompany the victims. They get tired. Sharing the emotion of the tragic moment, yes, everyone wants more and social networks are full of fiery flights for Simone Veil, the Queen of England or Pope Benedict, and then? And then we move on. The refusal of the equation of pain and time is the ultimate form of violence, and this time there is no one to hear.

"You're getting us drunk..."

I hate to say I'm a victim. I never say it. But I have to admit that, on a Karpman triangle[80], my place is systematically that of a victim. Like all victims, I hate the idea of being a victim. In the case of abduction, as in the case of sexual and gender-based violence, as in the case of racism or manipulation... those who claim the status of victim from the outset are the executioners. My mother, Noury, Mouloud, Yemma, Younous, my aunts, my uncles... all of them, at some point in history and in one way or another, present themselves as victims. And the idea revolts me. I hate the idea that I am a victim, but I hate even more that our society recognizes victims so badly, as it recognizes so badly the elderly or people affected by a handicap; or rather that it recognizes them as objects of compassion, as fodder for whining, delivered to the deadly agents of emotion, for as long as the emotion lasts... *Ah! the poor girl, what a destiny, how hard it is...* But who is going to be involved in the long run? Who will listen - again and again - to the violence suffered? Who to repair? My pain has only a spectacular value, demonstrative, psychologically indispensable

---

80.Dramatic triangle based on the transactional analysis of the psychologist Stephen Karpman, which shows a relationship between the three characters of the classic scheme of manipulation: victim, persecutor, rescuer.

to a public in search of anthropological reassurance at the spectacle of the misfortune of others. But who cares what I become? My close friends, my family, my shrinks sometimes... they all tell me that I need to "turn the page"... We turn the page of a divorce, a loss, a dismissal... but how do we turn my page? Of course it is too heavy. So I have to live with it. To live anyway, to live again, even with this taste of death.

To be recognized in the depth of my pain, that is my dream. No doubt this will be achieved through a lasting and indelible testimony. A book. It also means talking and listening over the long term. It also requires the consideration of those around me. As I said, this is the hardest part. The people around the victims, in a more or less short time according to the trauma, always end up minimizing the suffering experienced by the victim. All victims know the terrible moment when their case, when it has interested them for a moment, ceases to trigger sympathy to provoke boredom, indifference or hostility. A term has even been coined to explain this attitude of withdrawal, to relieve the guilt of the selfish: victimization, which would be a kind of social position of claiming status or compensation, because of the trauma suffered. One can understand the cynicism of the institution that makes this diagnosis; it conceals its blindness, its incompetence or, more simply, its intention to do nothing for the victims... who should, one suspects, "forget and move on". In the family or friendship circle, it is a matter of hiding one's own inaction, of denying the victim a recognition that will give him or her a place and rights in the family or friendship universe; often it is a matter of hiding one's mistakes, one's faults, and, in this case, the condemnation of the victim can even go beyond the simple refusal to consider him or her as such. The character played by Virginie Efira in *Revoir Paris* finds herself accused of a horrible act[81]... by the very person who committed this act, who thus makes a projection in order to lie to herself, to bury her "crime" by accusing another. My close family always minimized what had happened to me, each one skilfully or less skilfully shifting their responsibilities onto the other, all agreeing on the idea that "well, now we have to move on" and especially that I had my share of responsibility: the letter, the confessions to the police, my insolent attitude... I heard these words in my aunt's mouth: "She didn't deserve that, obviously, but hey...", a bit like they would have said of Charb and Cabu: "They didn't deserve that, obviously, but hey..."

On spring break of 2012, for example, at my sister Rose's house, I try to break that silence. I was asked to come, but I am there because my sister is there and I hope, without really believing it, that they will do me some justice. Mouloud and Alice are there, I find them very complicit. And suddenly, it comes out of me:

"Why is it that in the seventeen years I have been back, not one of you has given me half an hour to listen to what I have experienced? Why has no one asked me where I live, if I have a roof over my head, if I have food to eat, if I am happy, if I am beaten, if I am sad... if I go to school, if I am veiled, raped... Why does no one help me? Why can't I talk about my unhappiness? Not with you or even with my boyfriend? Mouloud, why do you say that I am your daughter but you don't help me? And Alice, you are my aunt, why have you always closed your eyes? You came to the bled with your son and your husband; I know you were afraid that your husband would do the same to your son,

____

81.Another woman who was present at the attack accuses her of having taken refuge in the toilet and of having closed the door to prevent others from hiding there. At the end of the film, she confesses her "mistake" but there remains the ambiguity of her level of awareness of the denial, the transference, and the accusation made.

18. Lifetime reconstruction

you told me so yourself, so that means you were capable enough to imagine what I was going through!"

They got a refill and went into the garden. There was a barbecue. It was the only time I got to tell them some of their dirty truths to their faces.

Anaïs told me several times that "the basis of [my] reconstruction is to grant [myself] the status of victim", to recognize it in order to be able to take stock of the damage. She is obviously right, and it is my responsibility to carry out this work. But having been absolutely objectified for so many years does not imply that my reconstruction is limited to the social recognition of my victim status. Being a victim will only be a part of my identity, a part that does not fully constitute me as a subject. I am much more than a victim, I am Marie-Claire.

19.
My letter

A free woman, Dad, you wanted me to be a free woman. That's why, you said to me, melancholic and disillusioned: "I made you in France, with a French woman, in the land of freedom. In my Algerian prison, you encouraged me to the extent of your small means: "Escape, leave, return and never come back." I know your cowardice, I forgave you. Laure, your granddaughter - who loves you so much from so far away - told me one day: you too were kidnapped by your own people who took everything from you while you were alive, even your identity which bothered them so much, just like me... We had the same executioners, and the same prison.

Dad, I have missed you since I was born. I have received your love beyond your absence. Sometimes I feel as if I have only known a shadow of you, a ghost. When I look at the ten yellowed photos of the handsome and muscular man you were, I feel an incurable sadness that I never knew the man you were before she betrayed you too, before they all betrayed you. Your folly, daddy dearest, was to have given them your trust and your love in the first place. They trampled on them, in the name of their infamous honor.

Dad, your granddaughter - whom you never knew but who wanted to start the process of bringing you to France, to your home, before death took you away - your granddaughter is asking me: "But why not write to her? And while we're at it, why not write to Annie too? The written word stays with you!Strange, I had never thought of that. It was a risk, the risk of reopening wounds of hate or love. And then I didn't have her address, nor yours, and I didn't want to see the adults of my childhood again, for fear of being like them perhaps… Her? I didn't want to see her, hear her or think about her, so I wrote to her… and why?

But "to write is not to reconnect", said Laure. I just had to write to deposit my story in words of black ink, indelible. You were right, my angel. But where to start?

It is a monstrous task to write to the one who inadvertently gave me life and death in cold blood. And now my co-author suggests that I write a letter to my parents to end our story. Even my friend Marine, my *sister*, jumped in, "Yesssss, I love the idea!"

The first question that came to me is childish but it torments me: how did you manage, Annie, not to love me even a little? I loved you, was I so repulsive? so hateful? How does one resist the love of one's child? What strange object was I in your eyes? What did I represent? Your failure ? Your hatred of the world? Your stupidity and your ignorance? Me, responsible for your mistakes and misfortunes? No matter how hard I try to understand you, I can't. For a long time, I wanted to look for - and find - what I called (damn cognitive dissociation) "circumstances of understanding", and I even invented some through abracadabratic detours: you had tried to protect me, maybe even from yourself, you felt incapable, others prevented you… or drugs, alcohol, what do I know? In reality, I did not find any. You have exhausted my being, my soul, my body, even my vocabulary in this search! I accept it now, Annie: I don't know who you are, I don't know you, neither the wife nor the mother. I don't know what it means to be someone's child, I thought for so long that I was the evil one.

What is it to have a mother? What is childhood? In the hell that you made me live, I believed for a long time that childhood means being guilty of existing and, for this very existence, deserving the torment of which you were the executor. Insulted, beaten, drowned, strangled, sold to the devil, denied, martyred, abandoned, killed more surely than Sethe's child, in Toni Morrison's beautiful novel[82] which tells the story of the ghost of a child who has come back to haunt her mother's house to demand an explanation. I too have come back from the dead to demand an explanation. But if I imagine with pain the tragedy of *Beloved*'s mother who slits her child's throat to break the chain of transmission of slavery, I have, on the other hand, nothing but contempt for the baseness of the ideas that led you to sell me as a slave to the cutters.

I know that you were a child, I know that you knew nothing about life or love, I know that society demands children, I know that you can regret losing your life because you did not know how to say no to the pressures of the world. I know that... But why didn't you just drop me at the door of a home or a hospital? How many times, against my will and my nature, have I thought that it would have been better to be thrown in a garbage can or left on a deserted beach at high tide, like in the terrible Alice Diop film[83] that I just saw, than to give myself up to this life of darkness?

The truth is written here in this book where I deposit my traumas, forever. It has resurrected me from the death you gave me anyway.

How do you decide to organize the abduction of your child, Mom?

The chain of endless, interlocking questions is endless. There is so much to say that there is nothing left to say. Faced with your denial, your refusal of dialogue, my choice is to live in reality, the truth, my

82. Toni Morrison, *Beloved*, 10/18, Foreign Domain, Pulitzer Prize 1987.
83. *Saint-Omer*, Alice Diop, 2022.

freedom. When I returned, you continued to lie, minimize, deny, cheat. Thank you, mama spider a la Louise Bourgeois, it almost killed me again but, you see, it made me stronger. For a long time I refused to cry, then the tears came. They were of frozen blood. They did not free me, so I stopped crying. You and your accomplices made Dad and me your sufferers, but I stopped being your object, your victim. The blood of my family has the color and the smell of the one that the murderers and the executioners shed. This, Annie, is what I know. Your violence has wandering as its center of gravity. I leave you there. Neither courage nor luck, nor even hell or redemption, I wish you nothing, Annie. I don't know who you are but I don't care. For me, you died over forty years ago. I stay with Dad's love.

Dad, I love you, rest in peace. Today, mom died, or maybe yesterday already...

Epilogue

Paris, October 13, 2022

Gloomy sky and light drizzle. 7 am. "...the pain of living, that it is necessary to live, worth living..." I listen to Barbara to escape Paris which wakes up with horns and snoring engines. In front of me, two men agitate around the tubulars of a market which settles. I step back. I'm always afraid of being pushed around. Walking towards the metro, I avoid the sewer gutters and the brooms of the cafetiers. See you at the hospital. A small operation of nothing at all, but it adds to the rotten autumn and my morale.

Between Chaussée-d'Antin and Place-Monge, Barbara suits my mood. I scroll through my "Rapture" folder on my phone. I have compiled several messages from children in abduction situations around the world. When I'm feeling blue or too dead in the throat, I scroll through the messages and I end up telling myself that I can still be useful to these forgotten people.

K. "Good evening, congratulations for your association, it was my father who brought me back to Algeria for my own good, I was 14 years old, I am 52 today. I regret not having had the courage to fight.

M. "Hello, I was born in France, my father made us go back to Morocco for a vacation in 1997, what are the steps to get French nationality and leave, please?"

N. "I was at the DDASS, my biological mother kidnapped me during a visit and she brought me to Algeria to her family and then returned to France. She was never convicted. I want to return. How do I do that?"

A. "I have not been able to escape, I have been struggling for more than 30 years, today I have three children but I still hope to return to France..."

F. "My sister was repatriated [...] she went through monstrous stages [...] she is homeless in Egypt..."

Z. "I just saw your testimony on the networks, I was also abducted by my genitress when I was 10 years old. We flew without an ID card for me. After a few years, fortunately my father found me and came to get me."

F. "I saw your video, I'm an educator, I've known cases like that, you need to write a book, I'll share it everywhere..."

G. "Hi, I've been in..."

Place-Monge. This is my station. This time, reading all these messages does not have the usual effect on me. Immensity of the task? Powerlessness? Too much time ? Loneliness ?

My phone vibrates. It's Pearl. "I made it to the embassy. My birth certificate has arrived." I look up at the white enamel sky at Exit 1 of Line 7 and search for the air deep in my lungs. I smile to myself, "It's just a step, beautiful. But trust me, one day you'll be on a plane to Paris. And I will be at the airport waiting for you."

Afterword

It is often said that the child we once were never dies. For Marie-Claire, it seems to me that it could never have existed. The Latin root of the word "child" is enlightening in this sense: "child" comes from the Latin "*infans*," meaning "who does not speak". In contemporary society, the consideration of the child as an individual with rights is relatively recent.

In Roman law, the child did not exist as a subject of law but remained the property of his or her progenitor, the *pater familias*. Later, in the old French law, the child was considered under the sole prism of the transmission of the family patrimony. The family succession gave him rights. It was not until the nineteenth and twentieth centuries that a paradigm shift took place, even if the child was considered more as an object of education than as a free subject. However, the last few decades have seen a profound change in the recognition of the need to protect the child. The child has become a subject of law in its own right, with social, economic and cultural rights, but above all with freedom. A multitude of texts of different nature and scope concern the illicit movement of children, but here only a few - the most effective - will be mentioned.

The International Convention on the Rights of the Child, adopted on November 20, 1989 by the United Nations General Assembly and ratified by one hundred and ninety-six countries, is now one of the major legal instruments. This text aims to guarantee every child, without exception, respect for his or her rights and protection against all forms of discrimination, and obliges States parties not only to work towards, but above all to take positive measures to promote respect for their rights. The Convention defines a child as "every human being below the age of eighteen years unless he or she attains majority earlier" (art. 1), thus leaving aside the subjective assessment that the child does not have the right to speak. Thus, the convention protects, inter alia, the right of a child to know and be cared for by his or her parents (Art. 7); the right to preserve his or her identity, including nationality, name and family relations (Art. 8); the right not to be separated from his or her parents against his or her will, except when necessary in the best interests of the child (Art. 9); and the right of a child with understanding to express his or her views freely in all matters affecting the child (Art. 12). Above all, the Convention provides in article 11 that States parties are required to take measures to combat the illicit transfer and non-return of children abroad and, to this end, to promote the conclusion of bilateral or multilateral agreements or accession to existing agreements. A total of ninety-six countries have ratified this convention. Among them, France in 1990 and Algeria in 1993.

Other international, community and national texts complete the legal arsenal aimed at promoting and protecting children's rights.

The Hague Convention of 25 October 1980 concludes on the civil aspects of international child abduction. This convention aims to protect children from the harmful effects of wrongful removal and retention across international borders by providing for an immediate return procedure and guaranteeing the protection of access rights. Article 3 of the Convention provides that "the removal or retention of a child shall be considered wrongful if: (a) it is in breach of rights of custody attributed to a person, an institution or any other body, either jointly or alone, under the law of the State in which the child was habitually resident immediately before the removal or retention; and (b) those rights were actually exercised, either jointly or alone, at the time of removal or retention, or would have been so exercised but for the removal or retention. The right of custody referred to in (a) may arise, inter alia, by operation of law, by judicial or administrative decision, or by an agreement in force under the law of that State. To date, one hundred and three States, including France, are parties to the Convention, which entered into force on 1 December 1983.

At the same time, the new "Brussels II ter" regulation, concerning jurisdiction, recognition and enforcement of judgments in matrimonial matters, parental responsibility and international child abduction, is applicable as of August 1, 2022. The latter now insists on the necessary speed of the procedure (art. 24), since it is provided that the courts seized must render their decision within six weeks, a decision that is also based on taking into account the child's opinion. Thus, Article 21 of the Regulation states that the courts of the Member States shall, in accordance with their laws and procedures, give a child who is capable of forming his or her own views a real and effective opportunity to express them. When the court gives a child the opportunity to express his or her views, it must give due weight to the views of the child in accordance with his or her age and degree of maturity.

There are also bilateral conventions, in particular the convention between Algeria and France concerning the children of separated Franco-Algerian mixed couples, created in Algiers on June 21, 1988 and which came into force in France on August 1, 1988. However, it only applies to children considered legitimate, i.e. born after marriage according to Algerian family law. The purpose of these bilateral conventions is to promote judicial cooperation between the countries in order to ensure an immediate return.

In theory, international and Community provisions must be transposed into French law to be applicable in France. However, these provisions are of such importance that the French judge can directly take them into account.

Also, internal mechanisms, facilitating the implementation of these instruments, are available to applicants.

On the one hand, each signatory country must have a central authority responsible for fulfilling the obligations imposed by the Hague Convention (Art. 6). In France, this authority is represented by the Bureau of European Union Law, Private International Law and Mutual Assistance in Civil Matters (Bureau du droit de l'Union, du droit international privé et de l'entraide civile) of the Directorate of Civil Affairs and Seals (Direction des affaires civiles et du sceau - DACS) of the Ministry of Justice. It can be contacted by post, telephone, fax or e-mail. The request must be accompanied by several documents attesting to the situation and the existence of this right (judgment, civil status certificate, certificate etc.). When the application is submitted by the applicant, DACS may agree to assist and forward the application to the requested Contracting State for a decision on the immediate return of the child. In practice, it is the holder of custody rights who can refer the matter to the Central Authority of the child's State of origin or refuge, i.e. the parent. Recourse to the DACS is not compulsory and the applicant can directly refer to the judicial authorities.

On the other hand, the public prosecutor to whom the request for immediate return is referred takes all the necessary steps to ensure the voluntary return of the child. To this end, he has investigative powers and must communicate certain elements of the investigation to the DACS. He may also order any expertise or examination that he deems necessary.

Finally, the family court judge rules on requests for a ban on the child leaving French territory without the parents' authorization and may liaise with the children's judge, particularly in the case of educational assistance proceedings.

In any event, there are four exceptions to the immediate return of the child. Firstly, if more than one year has elapsed between the removal of the child and the referral to the court, and the child has settled in his or her new environment; secondly, in case of non-exercise of custody rights, acquiescence or consent to the removal or non-return, even if this is later; thirdly, if there is a serious risk that the return will place the child in a situation of physical or psychological danger, or in an intolerable situation; fourthly, in the event of refusal by the child of sufficient age and maturity.

A legal arsenal then. A legal arsenal that has been thought through, matured, improved, tested, but not all-powerful.

Marie-Claire's testimony is edifying in this sense. How could such a situation have continued and become necrotic for so many years? Above all, if we go back to the root of the problem, how in France, despite multiple scenes of abuse known to all, did this man manage to leave the country with a minor child over whom he had no legal authority? It is in this respect that the story of Marie-Claire strongly questions this notion of "authority".

"I belong to everyone but myself," says Marie-Claire.

At what age should a child's opinion be taken into account? Why, even though Marie-Claire verbalizes her condition and the situation of extreme danger in which she finds herself, is she not listened to? It is certain that her story testifies to a violent negation of her condition as a right-holder. If the above-mentioned conventions aim at giving back a real and effective voice to children (cf. art. 21 of the *Brussels* II ter *regulation*), the fact remains that the tendency remains to mistrust, since the word of the child can be instrumentalized.

A more symbolic reading of these legal texts highlights one fact: the applicant who applies to the DACS is the holder of custody rights, i.e. the person legally responsible. The question of proof of the child's integration in the State of refuge falls to the parent who has moved the child, and the methods of hearing the child and taking his or her opinion into account remain at the discretion of the States. Moreover, the analysis of exceptions to the return of the child is often seen from the point of view of the parent and not of the child. Under these conditions, it seems legitimate to question the real place of the minor.

Furthermore, what recourse does the child have when parents fail to act? In law, and in general, the participation of the child in the decisions that concern him or her is subordinated to his or her faculty of discernment, age or degree of maturity. However, these notions are not defined and leave a subjective margin of appreciation to the Member States. In reality, this much deeper problem questions the perception of the child in our societies, a question that is all the more thorny as it varies from country to country and depends on the societal context. These differences of appreciation create disparate situations, sources of discrimination and legal insecurity. Thus, the effectiveness of judicial cooperation can be undermined or even reduced to nothing.

In the story of Marie-Claire, this is obvious. When she was taken to Algeria in the summer of 1985, an agreement on cooperation and mutual legal assistance between France and Algeria had been in force since October 1, 1980. According to this agreement, "the Ministries of Justice shall assist each other in the search for and location of children whose custody rights are disputed or unknown. They shall comply with requests for information concerning the material and moral situation of such children. They shall assist each other in obtaining the voluntary surrender of such children through conciliation. The child and his or her moral situation seem to be at the heart of the concerns of both countries. However, the episode of her meeting with the French Prime Minister of the time, who asked her if she wished to return to France in the presence of her torturers, is disarming.

In reality, as Marie-Claire points out in her story, the battle is not on equal terms. She is only a child, then a teenager, then a woman in a patriarchal society. In theory, her condition as a child and then as a woman should not be problematic since she has rights, like everyone else. In practice, the effectiveness of these rights is undermined. In reality, she is vulnerable and at the mercy of her torturers. Nothing is done administratively or judicially to facilitate her task, and it is easy to imagine the difficulties these children have in asserting their rights, if they even know them!

In addition, the question of the training of professional actors is important. Psychologists, doctors, magistrates, lawyers, investigators, educators, social workers, teachers, all need to be trained. Even if the trend towards specialization of magistrates in charge of these issues is to be welcomed, the establishment of an adequate framework for the collection of the child's word at all stages of the procedure is urgent. All the more so in view of the conflict of loyalty that is at stake for the child. For this, a multidisciplinary approach must be adopted and obviously, in parallel, material and human means must be granted. This training would necessarily allow to reduce the risk of instrumentalization of the child's word.

In any case, for Marie-Claire and for all the children who are victims of parental abduction and uprooting, it is essential to include in the notion of the best interests of the child the idea that "no one can really speak for the abducted children, no one but themselves, and it is such a long way to free up that word.

Master Anaïs BIEHLER

Table of contents

Best sellers Max Milo Editions

Hitler's banker, Jean-François Bouchard

Confessions of a forger, Éric Piedoie Le Tiec

The Koran and the flesh, Ludovic-Mohamed Zahed

Governing by fake news, Jacques Baud

Governing by chaos, Collectif

A political history of food, Paul Ariès

Mad in U.S.A.: The ravages of the "American model",
Michel Desmurget

Mondial soccer club geopolitics, Kévin Veyssière

Putin: Game master?, Jacques Braud

Treatise on the three impostors: Moses, Jesus, Muhammad,
The Spirit of Spinoza

TV Lobotomy, Michel Desmurget

www.ingramcontent.com/pod-product-compliance
Lightning Source LLC
LaVergne TN
LVHW021603060726
842527LV00015B/3899